aircraft that never flew in Afghanistan and two more aircraft involved in DEA missions out of Fort Lauderdale, Florida; (2) training for DEA and contract personnel who never went to Afghanistan; and (3) travel-related to missions in Port Au Prince, Haiti; the Bahamas; Lima, Peru; and Florida that was unrelated to the DEA's aviation operations in Afghanistan. Additionally, we determined that the DEA charged $78,208 to the MOUs in unsupported non-personnel costs. The DEA also diverted $1,664,699 in funds from these MOUs for maintenance of the Global Discovery ATR 500 aircraft, travel to oversee the Global Discovery program, and training for pilots and mechanics to fly the ATR 500. Since these MOUs were intended to support ongoing operations with the Beech King Air 350s prior to deployment of the ATR 500, the DEA's expenditures on the Global Discovery program are unallowable and, as previously stated, the ATR 500 has never been deployed or operated in Afghanistan.

We found that the DEA did not ensure that the MOUs it entered into with the DOD contained clear objectives and deliverables. Therefore, it is not clear what the DEA was supposed to accomplish with its two aircraft in Afghanistan. In the absence of any established deliverables, we reviewed the DEA's quarterly reports submitted to the DOD of missions flown and missions declined and then compared them to the DEA's mission report data. We determined that for each of the 10 quarters we reviewed, the DEA inaccurately reported this information to the DOD. We also found that only 14 percent of the missions that the DEA flew in Afghanistan between October 2011 and February 2015 were for reconnaissance, surveillance, and intelligence, while 79 percent were for transporting personnel and equipment. Additionally, between February 2012 and January 2015, the DEA received more than 1,000 mission requests in Afghanistan that it could not fulfill and, at the DEA's request, between October 2011 and May 2015 the State Department flew 1,223 missions for general aviation support of DEA operations. We also determined that the only operational DEA surveillance aircraft had been removed from Afghanistan in October 2012, for approximately 8 months, without providing a substitute aircraft in Afghanistan, which further compounded the DEA's inability to provide aviation support. Without deliverables and an accurate method to track and report performance, the DEA was unable to determine if it was effectively meeting its operational needs and goals. However, based on the data available to us, our findings raise serious questions as to whether it was doing so. Finally, we have referred all findings relating to the DOD's oversight of the Global Discovery program to the DOD Office of Inspector General.

We make 13 recommendations to the DEA to assist in improving its management and oversight of its MOUs for aviation operations and the Global Discovery program.

AUDIT OF THE DRUG ENFORCEMENT ADMINISTRATION'S AVIATION OPERATIONS WITH THE DEPARTMENT OF DEFENSE IN AFGHANISTAN

EXECUTIVE SUMMARY

In fiscal year 2008 the Drug Enforcement Administration (DEA) expended nearly $8.6 million to purchase an ATR 42-500 aircraft (ATR 500) to support its counternarcotics efforts in Afghanistan. The Department of Defense (DOD) agreed to modify the DEA's ATR 500 with surveillance equipment and other capabilities to conduct such operations in the combat environment of Afghanistan in what became known as the Global Discovery program. In addition, through five Memoranda of Understanding (MOU) with the DOD, between fiscal years 2012 and 2015, the DEA received $29,080,137 from the DOD to support both the DEA's counternarcotics aviation operations in Afghanistan and the Global Discovery program. As of February 2015, the DEA had expended $10.1 million of this funding for the Global Discovery aircraft. The DOD has also expended an additional $67.9 million in DOD appropriated funds to modify the DEA's ATR 500 and to construct a hangar at the Kabul International Airport in Afghanistan for the aircraft. Even though collectively the DEA and DOD have spent more than $86 million on the Global Discovery program, we found that, over 7 years after the aircraft was purchased for the program, the aircraft remains inoperable, resting on jacks, and has never actually flown in Afghanistan.

The Department of Justice Office of the Inspector General (OIG) initiated an audit of the DEA's Global Discovery program and operations under the MOUs with the DOD based on a whistleblower complaint alleging that the DEA misused DOD funds by misdirecting, diverting, and spending them in areas not related to DEA's Afghanistan aviation operations. Our audit objectives were to assess the DEA's Global Discovery program and its compliance with the MOUs that the DEA entered into with the DOD for supporting DEA's aviation operations in Afghanistan. Our findings include the following:

- The Global Discovery program began in September 2008 with the purchase of the ATR 500 and was originally intended to be completed in December 2012, but it has missed every intended delivery date that has been established. The program has cost almost four times its original anticipated amount of $22 million and the DEA's ATR 500 was still not operational as of March 2016.

- The DEA did not fully comply with the Federal Acquisition Regulation (FAR) and its own solicitation in purchasing the aircraft. Specifically, we found that the DEA did not ensure that legitimate needs were identified and trade-offs evaluated, as required by the FAR, to ensure that the aircraft being purchased met operational needs in the most cost-effective manner. As a result, the Aviation Division did not take into account, when purchasing the ATR 500, the time and cost it would incur to establish an infrastructure of pilots, mechanics, trainers, and spare parts required to operate the aircraft compared to the cost of leveraging its existent fleet infrastructure.

- The DEA also failed to evaluate, as required by the FAR, each bid received on all the factors it listed in its solicitation. Therefore, the DEA ultimately awarded a contract for the purchase of an aircraft that cost $3 million more than it had estimated, even though that aircraft potentially did not best meet the DEA's technical needs and performance requirements.

Given these issues, we question the DEA's procurement of the aircraft for $8,572,638 because it did not fully adhere to federal acquisition regulations and was never used for the purposes for which it was procured. Our findings go beyond these fundamental flaws in the acquisition of the aircraft, and extend to the deficiencies in the handling of issues that arose as the Global Discovery program failed to move forward. These include the following:

- In March 2012, the DEA transferred the ATR 500 to a DOD aircraft maintenance subcontractor with no formal record of the transfer of possession and without entering into an MOU with the DOD for the Global Discovery program. Without an MOU, the DEA has had difficulty ensuring that all agreed upon modifications were made and holding the DOD accountable for timely completion of the project.

- In December 2012, while the Global Discovery program missed its initial delivery date, the DOD had awarded a contract in the amount of $1.9 million for a replacement hangar to be built for the DEA at Camp Alvarado, located at the Kabul International Airport, specifically to house the ATR 500. Yet, as the modifications continued, this hangar never housed the Global Discovery aircraft. In July 2015, the DEA removed its aviation operations from Afghanistan and the ATR 500 will most likely never be housed in the hangar.

- By October 2014, the Global Discovery program had missed four more delivery dates and ran out of money. The DOD considered scrapping the aircraft because, while the DOD had already expended more than $65.9 million on the aircraft's modifications, an additional $6 million was required to repair damages observed during attempts to modify the aircraft. Yet, at that time, the market value of the ATR 500 was only $6 million.

- DEA and DOD officials estimate that the ATR 500 will not be completed with all agreed upon modifications. For instance, a retractable camera system will be fix-mounted and a radar system will not be included in the modification to the aircraft as planned, leaving the DEA to arrange for its installation at a cost estimated at an additional $3 million.

- As of March 2016, modification efforts remain on-going, and the most recent delivery date provided for an operable ATR 500 is June 2016.

Our audit also questioned $2,461,401 in unallowable and unsupported expenditures charged by the DEA to three of the four MOUs with the DOD that were intended to support the DEA's two Beech King Air 350s operating in Afghanistan until the deployment of the Global Discovery ATR 500. Specifically, we found that the DEA charged $718,494 to the MOUs, including: (1) maintenance costs for one

AUDIT OF THE DRUG ENFORCEMENT ADMINISTRATION'S AVIATION OPERATIONS WITH THE DEPARTMENT OF DEFENSE IN AFGHANISTAN

TABLE OF CONTENTS

AUDIT OF THE DRUG ENFORCEMENT ADMINISTRATION'S AVIATION OPERATIONS WITH THE DEPARTMENT OF DEFENSE IN AFGHANISTAN

INTRODUCTION

We performed an audit of the Drug Enforcement Administration's (DEA) Global Discovery program and its Memoranda of Understanding (MOU) with the Department of Defense (DOD) to support DEA aviation operations in Afghanistan.[1] The purpose of the Global Discovery program was for the DEA to purchase one ATR 42-500 aircraft (ATR 500) and retrofit it with advanced surveillance equipment and transport capabilities to support the DEA's counternarcotics operations in Afghanistan. Funding for these DEA efforts was received through two sources, DEA's direct appropriation, which was used to purchase the ATR 500 for nearly $8.6 million in fiscal year 2008, and five MOUs with the DOD for $29,080,137, which was used to purchase parts for the ATR 500 and to more generally support DEA aviation operations in Afghanistan.[2] As of February 2015, the DEA had spent $30,370,676 (81 percent) of this combined funding.

We also determined that the DOD separately expended an additional $67.9 million of its own appropriated funds toward the cost of modification, and to build a hangar for the plane at Camp Alvarado, located at the Kabul International Airport, to house the ATR 500 for use in Afghanistan. Thus, as of July 2015, in total, the DEA and DOD have spent more than $86 million in appropriated funds on the ATR 500.

---

[1] Pub. L. No. 101-510 (1990) provides the DOD with the statutory authority to provide support to federal law enforcement agencies to establish and operate bases for counternarcotics operations in foreign countries.

MOUs are interagency agreements used to enter into contracts with other federal, state, or local entities in order to exchange goods and services. Under the U.S. Economy Act, the DEA is authorized to enter into both incoming and outgoing reimbursable agreements (RA) with other federal entities.

[2] Pub. L. No. 110-28 (2007) appropriated $8,468,000 in emergency supplemental funding to the DEA for salaries and expenses for FY 2007 to remain available until September 30, 2008. DEA officials informed us that this supplemental funding along with $104,638 appropriated from the DEA's budget was used to purchase the ATR 500.

Table 1

Funding for the Global Discovery Program

Fiscal Year/s	Source of Funding	Purpose	Expended
2008	DEA Direct Appropriations	Purchase of ATR 500	$8,572,638
2013	DOD Direct Appropriations	Hangar built to house ATR 500	$1,855,990
2013	DEA MOUs with DOD	ATR 500 parts	$8,467,591
2012-2015		Aviation Operations in Afghanistan (Unallowable charges)	$1,664,699
2010-2014	DOD Direct Appropriations	ATR 500 modifications	$65,998,242
		Total	**$86,559,160**

Source: DEA and DOD

Background

Through surveillance activities, photographic reconnaissance, and fugitive, prisoner and cargo transportation, the DEA's Aviation Division supports the DEA's mission to enforce the controlled substances laws and regulations of the United States domestically and abroad. The Aviation Division has approximately 125 Special Agent Pilots and nearly 100 aircraft in locations across the U.S., Caribbean, Central and South America, and Afghanistan. Aviation operations are coordinated and overseen from the Aviation Operations Center in Fort Worth, Texas, which serves as the primary maintenance facility for DEA's fleet of aircraft, as well as headquarters for its supervisory, administrative, and contract personnel.

Whistleblower Allegation

In a July 2014 letter to the Inspector General, the U.S. Office of Special Counsel conveyed allegations that it received from an anonymous source regarding the misuse of government funds by the DEA. Specifically, the whistleblower complaint alleged that the DEA misused DOD funds that were intended to support the DEA's counternarcotics aviation operations in Afghanistan by misdirecting, diverting, and spending the money for purposes unrelated to the DEA's Afghanistan aviation operations. This whistleblower allegation led us to initiate this audit.

DEA's Operations in Afghanistan

According to the DEA, its mission in Afghanistan is to: (1) deny narcotic-generated funding to terrorists and insurgents, (2) break the nexus between the insurgency and drug trafficking, (3) promote the rule of law, (4) expose and reduce corruption, and (5) diminish the overall drug threat from Afghanistan. After it was closed in 1979 due to the Soviet invasion, the DEA reopened its Kabul Country Office in 2003, which operates out of the U.S. Embassy in Kabul, Afghanistan. In 2013, the DEA had a total of 97 authorized permanent positions and 13 contractor positions in Afghanistan. DEA personnel are augmented by the Counternarcotics

Police of Afghanistan.[3] The DEA told us that since it reopened the Kabul Country Office, it has disrupted 39 drug trafficking organizations and dismantled 10 organizations. In FY 2013, the DEA's budget for Afghanistan operations was approximately $58.6 million.[4]

Since 2008, the DEA's aviation operations have been based at Camp Alvarado, located at the Kabul International Airport in Afghanistan. From FY 2012 to FY 2014, Aviation Division personnel in Afghanistan typically consisted of a Group Supervisor, three Special Agent pilots, and eight contract personnel (three pilots and five aircraft mechanics) provided to the DEA by its contractor L-3 Communications Vertex Aerospace, LLC (L-3). The DEA operated two Beech King Air 350 aircraft; one was equipped with surveillance capabilities and the other, which did not have surveillance capabilities, was utilized primarily for transporting personnel and equipment. Between FYs 2012 and 2014, the DEA received the majority of its funding for aviation operations in Afghanistan through MOUs with the DOD. Since 2012, the DEA's Aviation Division has received over $20 million from the DOD to support DEA counternarcotics efforts in Afghanistan. In July 2015, the DEA removed all aviation personnel, aircraft, and equipment from Afghanistan. At that time, an Aviation Division official stated that its withdrawal was consistent with the U.S. military's drawdown of troops in Afghanistan, and that without the military's presence the DEA cannot maintain aviation operations in Afghanistan. After the announcement in October 2015 that the U.S. military plans to keep approximately 5,500 troops in Afghanistan, a DEA official stated that the Aviation Division did not have any plans to return to Afghanistan.

Global Discovery Program

The Global Discovery program is a joint project between the DOD and the DEA. The purpose of the program is to modify one DEA transport aircraft and provide it with advanced surveillance capabilities for use within the combat environment of Afghanistan. The DEA and the DOD agreed that the aircraft modifications would be made and funded by the DOD. The DEA's Assistant Administrator approved the Global Discovery program's Concept of Operations in November 2010, which established both the DEA and the DOD as primary stakeholders for the Global Discovery program.[5] The Global Discovery program's Concept of Operations also stated that the DOD would provide program management and executive oversight of the Global Discovery program. The proposed modifications to the DEA's aircraft would include the purchase of special

---

[3] Established in 2003, the Counternarcotics Police of Afghanistan serve as a counternarcotics specialist force of the Afghan National Police, conducting counternarcotics investigations and operations throughout Afghanistan. As of November 2013 the Counternarcotics Police of Afghanistan had more than 2,500 personnel.

[4] Approximately $33.9 million of this funding came from the State Department, $15.3 million from the DOD; and the remaining $9.4 million came from the DEA's own appropriation.

[5] The Global Discovery program's Concept of Operations document was for planning and decision making purposes as well as to assist in the development of formal requirements; it was not a formal statement of work.

equipment to perform precision geo-location operations, electro-optical infra-red (EO/IR) video capability utilizing two high definition cameras, radar, and a self-protection threat adaptive countermeasures dispenser system.[6]

DEA MOUs with the DOD

Beginning in FY 2012, the DEA entered into MOUs with the DOD and received DOD funding to support DEA aviation operations in Afghanistan. In an April 2011 letter to the Deputy Assistant Secretary for Counternarcotics and Global Threats, the DEA's Assistant Administrator requested DOD funding for aviation operations in Afghanistan to identify illicit drug labs, support counternarcotics investigations, support the seizure of narcotics and weapons, and to transport U.S. and Afghan law enforcement personnel and equipment. Prior to this time, the U.S. Department of State (State Department) primarily funded DEA's aviation operations in Afghanistan, but declined to do so for FY 2012. Without DOD's funding, the Assistant Administrator stated that the DEA could not fund aviation operations in Afghanistan on its own and would have to remove DEA aircraft from Afghanistan. As shown in Table 2, since FY 2012 the DOD provided the DEA funding each fiscal year to continue aviation operations in Afghanistan.

Table 2

**DOD MOU Funding for
DEA's Aviation Operations in Afghanistan**

Fiscal Year	Amount
2012	$3,255,000
2013	$6,640,000
2014	$6,560,000
2015	$3,880,000
	Total $20,335,000

Source: DEA

DEA Contract with L-3 Communications Vertex Aerospace LLC

Since January 2008, the DEA has contracted with L-3 to provide support for its Aviation Division, including aircraft maintenance, training, and administrative support. The DEA's most recent contract with L-3 was a cost-plus-fixed-fee contract entered into in December 2012, with a 1-year base period and four 1-year option periods – with subsequent modifications, this contract had an estimated total value of $144 million as of September 2014.[7] Many of the services provided by L-3

---

[6] The ATR 500's modifications were to: (1) provide video surveillance using EO/IR cameras and a laser designation system to image standing and walking human contacts during daylight or moonless nighttime operations; (2) continuously track and monitor multiple contacts (vehicle or person) at once while providing near real-time information to multiple agencies; (3) intercept wireless communications; and (4) protect the aircraft from incoming radar and infrared homing missiles with a countermeasures dispenser system.

[7] A cost-plus-fixed-fee contract is a cost-reimbursement contract that provides for payment to the contractor of a negotiated fee that is fixed at the inception of the contract.

were paid for with funds provided to the DEA through the MOUs with the DOD. Under its contract with the DEA, L-3 provides program management, aircraft maintenance, training, inventory management, and administrative support for DEA's aircraft worldwide, including in Kabul, Afghanistan. For Afghanistan operations specifically, L-3 provided the DEA with contract pilots and mechanics, as well as services related to the maintenance of two DEA Beech King Air 350 aircraft stationed in Kabul.

OIG Audit Approach

The objective of our audit was to assess the DEA's Global Discovery program and compliance with the MOUs that the DEA entered into with the DOD supporting DEA's aviation operations in Afghanistan. Specifically, we evaluated how the DEA utilized DOD funding for both the Global Discovery program and its aviation operations in Afghanistan. The scope of this audit, unless otherwise stated, focused on DEA's aviation operations in Afghanistan from October 1, 2012, through November 1, 2014.

In determining whether the DEA properly used Global Discovery program funding, we assessed whether the DEA's procurement of the aircraft in 2008 was in compliance with the Federal Acquisition Regulation (FAR) and evaluated the DEA's methodology for selecting an aircraft for purchase. We also reviewed the DEA's costs associated with the Global Discovery program to ensure that the costs were allowable, supported, and in accordance with applicable laws, regulations, and terms and conditions of the MOUs. With the DEA being one of the two primary stakeholders in the Global Discovery program, we assessed the timeliness and reasonableness of the ATR 500 modification, the allowableness of expenditures, and whether expenditures were sufficiently supported. In order to perform our audit, we relied on the DOD to provide us information, but we did not assess the DOD's oversight, management, or its overall specific funding related to the Global Discovery program. We referred all findings related to DOD's oversight of the Global Discovery program to the DOD Office of Inspector General.

We also evaluated the DEA's compliance with the terms and conditions of the MOUs it entered into with the DOD for the support of aviation operations in Afghanistan. Our review of the MOUs consisted of: (1) assessing whether the DEA's activities were in compliance with the requirements and intent of the MOUs; (2) determining if the DEA was meeting the DOD's goals and objectives contained in the MOUs; and (3) reviewing the DEA's MOU costs spent for aviation operations in Afghanistan. Specifically, we reviewed the DEA's submission of financial and programmatic reports to the DOD, as these reports were the basis for the DEA's request for reimbursement. We also evaluated the DEA's aviation operations in Afghanistan to include the number of missions flown, the number of missions declined, and the DEA's aircraft availability.

FINDINGS AND RECOMMENDATIONS

We found that the DEA and the DOD have spent more than $86 million dollars to purchase and modify a DEA-owned aircraft with surveillance capabilities to support the DEA's counternarcotics efforts in Afghanistan. The Global Discovery program has missed every intended delivery date since the ATR 500 was purchased in September 2008, cost nearly 4 times its original anticipated amount of $22 million, and is currently in an un-flyable state. The aircraft has never flown in Afghanistan as originally intended and, because the DEA removed all aviation operations from Afghanistan in July 2015, it likely never will. Moreover, despite the DEA's withdrawal from Afghanistan, as of March 2016, the DOD continued to spend appropriated funds in an effort to make the aircraft operational and flyable.

In addition, the DEA did not fully comply with the FAR and its own procedures in the procurement of the ATR 500. We also determined that the DEA transferred possession of the aircraft to the DOD to perform modifications on the aircraft for more than 3 years without any formal agreement with the DOD to ensure timely completion of the modifications and oversight of the Global Discovery program. Further, the DEA has purchased approximately $8.5 million in parts for the ATR 500 that it cannot utilize until the modifications are complete and the aircraft has been made flyable. The expected completion date for the Global Discovery project is now June 2016.

Moreover, we determined that the DEA spent $2,461,401 in MOU funding from the DOD, which was intended to support the DEA's two Beech King Air 350's operating in Afghanistan, on unallowable and unsupported expenditures. For example, we found that the DEA charged $2,383,193 in Global Discovery program related expenditures, travel-related expenditures for non-Afghanistan operations, training unrelated to Afghanistan, and other unallowable expenditures. The DEA also charged $78,208 to the MOUs in unsupported expenditures. Finally, the DEA did not ensure that the MOUs it entered into with the DOD had clear objectives and deliverables in order to determine if the use of MOU funds had any impact on its counternarcotics mission in Afghanistan. Without established deliverables, and because the DEA did not accurately track its performance, the DEA was unable to perform a meaningful review and analysis of its operations to determine whether or not it was effectively assessing and meeting operational needs in Afghanistan.

Procurement of the Global Discovery Aircraft

In July 2008, the DEA placed a pre-solicitation notice on the Federal Business Opportunities website for the purchase of the aircraft that the DEA would later refer to as the Global Discovery aircraft. The notice indicated that the DEA was seeking to purchase an ATR 42-320 (ATR 320) or an ATR 500 aircraft through a firm-fixed-price contract as a small business set-aside and that the solicitation would be posted solely on the DEA's website later that same month.[8] The notice also specified the mission critical requirements of the aircraft as: (1) capable of accommodating 4 crew members and 42 passengers; (2) providing a cargo opening; (3) Federal Aviation Administration (FAA) certified; and (4) in serviceable condition with not more than 25,000 hours total time on the airframe and either engine. The DEA had estimated spending $5.8 million on the aircraft purchase and received six offers from two different companies. The offers received by the DEA included bids for two used ATR 42-300s that could be modified to a 320 standard, two used ATR 320s, and two used ATR 500s.

We have several concerns about the actions taken by the DEA in its solicitation and procurement process for the ATR aircraft. The FAR Part 6.302-1 states that a brand name specification may be selected when only one responsible source and no other supplies or services shall satisfy agency requirements. The DEA cited FAR Part 6.302-1 as the authority for its procurement of the brand name ATR aircraft. In addition, the FAR Part 6.302-1 (c) requires that a brand-name justification be posted with a solicitation to indicate only one particular brand name will satisfy agency requirements. Posting of a brand-name justification ensures that agencies are transparent about the reasons for limiting the use of brand names in order to demonstrate compliance with the FAR and promotes maximum competition, thereby helping to ensure that agencies are purchasing the best products to meet its agency needs. The DEA provided us with a brand-name justification that included a description of the ATR aircraft it sought to purchase. Specifically, the justification focused on DEA's established infrastructure for operating and maintaining the ATR 320 including: (1) 12 pilots qualified to operate the aircraft; (2) qualified instructors capable of conducting recurrent training on the aircraft; and (3) trained mechanics to work on the ATR 320. A DEA official also stated that it had taken 4 years and more than $300,000 to build the infrastructure for its ATR 320. The justification only discussed the DEA's established infrastructure for operating and maintaining an ATR 320, not the ATR 500, which the DEA ultimately purchased for the Global Discovery program. Moreover, the DEA did not post the brand-name justification with its solicitation.

Second, the FAR Part 10.001(a)(1) requires agencies to ensure that legitimate needs are identified and trade-offs are evaluated in order to acquire items that meet those needs. Although the DEA's procurement documents were based solely on the purchase of an ATR aircraft and an ATR 500 was ultimately procured, the DEA never evaluated the trade-offs between the two aircrafts listed in

---

[8] According to the FAR, Part 19.501, a small business set-aside is the reserving of an acquisition exclusively for participation by small business concerns and competition may be open to all small businesses.

In June 2008, the DEA posted a request for information on the Federal Business Opportunities website for a used ATR 320 or 500 twin-engine turbine powered passenger, cargo, and special mission aircraft.

its solicitation. Without evaluating the trade-offs between the ATR 320 and the ATR 500 it was unclear to us why the DEA determined that the ATR 500, an aircraft costing almost $3 million more than the DEA had estimated spending and for which the DEA did not have an established infrastructure, was the best fit for its operations. An Aviation Division official told the OIG that the selected ATR 500 was a newer aircraft than the ATR 320, provided superior performance, and that much of the infrastructure (pilots, mechanics, etc.) was transferrable to the ATR 500, allowing pilots and mechanics to easily shift between the two ATR's without much additional training. However, a DEA ATR pilot stated he would not want to fly the ATR 500 until he had received ATR 500 specific training. Without a needs assessment, as required by the FAR, the DEA did not evaluate the trade-offs involved with the purchase of either the ATR 320 or the ATR 500, to determine which aircraft would best meet its needs.

Third, the FAR Part 15.303(b)(4) provides that all bids are to be evaluated based on the factors and sub-factors contained in the solicitation. Once the bids were received, the DEA conducted a technical evaluation of each aircraft in order to make its decision. According to the solicitation, the DEA's technical evaluation was comprised of three factors with a combined total of 100 points and the scores for each bid would be determined by two Technical Evaluators.[9] The Technical Evaluators would give the top scoring bids a "Pass" or "Fail" rating on the first factor and, unless the bid received a pass on that score, it would not be further considered. However, despite DEA's technical evaluation plan, we found that the DEA did not evaluate any of the aircraft on all three factors as specified in the solicitation. Instead, the Technical Evaluators rated the bids based solely on Factor 1, even though it accounted for only half the specified scoring. The results of the technical evaluation as performed by the DEA are illustrated in Table 3.

---

[9] The DEA's three technical evaluation factors were broken down as: (1) 50 points for the amount of time flown on the airframe and the amount of time until required maintenance; (2) 25 points for the condition of the aircraft's interior and exterior; and (3) 25 points for all past required maintenance conducted and completed. These technical evaluation factors would then be weighed equally with the aircraft's purchase price.

Table 3

**DEA's Technical Evaluation for Procurement
of the Global Discovery Aircraft**

Company	Aircraft Offered(Manufacturer's Serial Number)	Offer Price	Factor 1 Technical Evaluation Score[a]	Pass/Fail based on Factor 1
Nordic Aviation Contractor A/S	Used ATR 300 MSN 022	$2,600,000	9	Fail
CSI Aviation Service, Inc.	Used ATR 320 MSN 139	$4,834,375[b]	19	Fail
Nordic Aviation Contractor A/S	Used ATR 320 MSN 257	$4,300,000	21	Fail
Nordic Aviation Contractor A/S	Used ATR 300 MSN 331	$5,200,000	24	Pass
CSI Aviation Services, Inc.	Used ATR 500 MSN 549	$8,588,965[b]	29	Pass
CSI Aviation Services, Inc.	Used ATR 500 MSN 614	$9,997,680	30	Pass

[a] The score is the average of the two Technical Evaluators scoring based on Factor 1.

[b] CSI's offer for aircraft MSNs 139 and 549 were provided to the DEA during negotiations that occurred prior to the technical evaluations and after the DEA's solicitation had closed on August 7, 2008. The original offer price of ATR MSN 549 was reduced by $16,327 to the DEA's final purchase price of $8,572,638.

Source: DEA

We asked a DEA official why it did not consider Factors 2 and 3 as part of its technical evaluation. The DEA official stated that Factors 2 and 3 were to be reviewed later during the inspection phase if the condition and quality of the aircraft was deemed suitable based on Factor 1. Even though three of the six aircraft received a "Pass" grade from the Technical Evaluators for Factor 1, a DEA official stated that only the ATR 500 rated a 29, was deemed suitable and would be rated on Factors 2 and 3.[10] A DEA official stated that the DEA's Quality Assurance Specialist, two L-3 mechanics, and a DEA pilot traveled to Denmark and Germany to perform on-site inspections of the ATR 500 and to rate it on Factors 2 and 3. While the DEA provided evidence that an inspection of the ATR 500 occurred prior to purchasing the aircraft, the DEA did not provide documentation that the ATR 500, or any of the bids received, were ever rated on Factors 2 and 3 as listed in the solicitation. Therefore, the DEA's contract for and purchase of the ATR 500 from CSI in the amount of $8,572,638 violated FAR requirements and the DEA is unable to show that the aircraft purchased best met its technical needs and performance requirements.

In response to this finding, the DEA stated that it improved its policy and procedures since it awarded CSI the contract in 2008. Specifically, in 2011 the DEA implemented its Standard Operating Acquisition Procedure, which created a formal process and procedures for providing oversight and advisory review of contract

---

[10] A DEA official stated that to save costs on traveling to inspect each aircraft on Factors 2 and 3, the DEA decided only to inspect the ATR 500 rated a 29. The ATR 500 rated a 30 was found to be too expensive and the ATR 300, was not the DEA's preferred ATR model.

actions by the DEA.[11] The DEA also established the Contract Review Board to ensure compliance with the FAR and other legal requirements, adherence to DEA and DOJ policy and procedural guidance, conformity to acquisition best practices, soundness of acquisition strategy, and allowance of competition to the maximum extent practicable. The DEA informed us that acquisitions exceeding $650,000, which would typically include aircrafts the DEA sought to purchase, are subject to routine review by the Contact Review Board. The review board includes the: (1) Section Chief; (2) Office of the Chief Counsel representative; (3) Unit Chief, Policy and Analysis Unit; (4) Contracting Officer responsible for the acquisition; and (5) any subject matter experts or other individuals needed on a case by case basis.

These are positive steps to ensure the proper oversight of its acquisitions. However, we take issue with the purchase of the ATR 500 for several reasons. The DEA did not: (1) ensure that legitimate needs were identified and trade-offs were evaluated, (2) post a brand-name justification with its solicitation, and (3) evaluate the bids submitted based on all factors listed in the solicitation. Therefore, we question the DEA's procurement of the ATR 500 aircraft for $8,572,638 and recommend that the DEA strengthen internal controls to ensure existing policies and procedures are followed and that it abides by the FAR in its solicitation and procurement process when purchasing future aircraft.

The Global Discovery Program

In fiscal year 2009, the DEA and the DOD began discussions for development of the Global Discovery program using the ATR 500 that the DEA acquired as set forth above. Both agencies had a mutual desire to enhance the DEA's aviation operations in Afghanistan, including aerial and ground reconnaissance capabilities. Specifically, the DOD wanted to leverage the Global Discovery program to combine the efforts of the DEA and DOD operating in Afghanistan in order to improve overall operational and strategic results.

---

[11] In April 1999, the DEA implemented a standardized contract file checklist to ensure adequate procurement documentation be maintained in each contract file. In February 2004, the DEA established a Procurement Review Committee and implemented procedures for solicitation and contract reviews.

Figure 1

DEA's ATR 500 at DOD's Subcontractor's Facility
April 2015

Source: OIG

Within the DOD, the Global Discovery program was overseen by the Deputy Assistant Secretary of Defense for Counternarcotics and Global Threats (DASD CN&GT) office and the Naval Sea Systems Command Naval Surface Warfare Center Crane Division (NSWC Crane) was the DOD program office selected to manage the program in May 2010.[12] NSWC Crane had previously awarded an indefinite delivery indefinite quantity (IDIQ) contract to Concurrent Technologies Corporation (CTC) and in September 2010 NSWC Crane issued technical instruction for the Global Discovery program to CTC under this IDIQ contract. The technical instruction outlined the original amount of funding for the program, approximately $16 million, and established the period of performance from September 2010 through December 2012. CTC was the original prime contractor for the Global Discovery program and the main subcontractor was Summit Aviation.

In 2010, DEA's Aviation Division worked with NSWC Crane to establish a System Requirements Document that defined the DEA's tactical control of the ATR 500 when deployed in Afghanistan, and explained the threshold and objective requirements for the modification of the aircraft. Then in September 2010, the DEA Aviation Division and DEA Kabul Country Office officials met with NSWC Crane and validated the System Requirements Document. In November 2010, the System Requirements Document, outlining the modifications to be made on the ATR 500, was approved by the DEA's Chief of Operations. The intended modifications of the ATR 500 included:

---

[12] The DOD's Counter Narcoterrorism Technology Program Office (CNTPO) was the first program office to oversee the Global Discovery program in FY 2009. The CNTPO is chartered by the DASD CN&GT office with a mission to develop, deploy, and provide technology and acquisition solutions to engage, disrupt, and deter drug and narcoterrorism operations around the world.

NSWC Crane is a Department of the Navy Working Capital Fund activity that operates on a reimbursable and break-even basis. It is authorized by statute, 10 U.S.C. §2208, to charge for the services it provides and is authorized by the general authority of the Economy Act 31 U.S.C. §1535 to provide those services.

- the ability to perform precision geo-location operations;

- electro-optical infra-red video capability, utilizing two MX-20 cameras;

- the integration of data within the DOD's Distributed Command Ground System architecture to improve information sharing among the DEA and DOD;

- ground search synthetic aperture radar with the ability to interface with the aircraft's sensors;

- air to ground radios providing up and down link of data and radio transmissions to and from the aircraft; and

- self-protection, threat adaptive countermeasures dispenser system.

At the end of FY 2010, the DOD had expended approximately $26.8 million for the purchase of sensors and the labor costs for research, development, and planning for integrating the sensors onto the ATR 500. However, it was not until January 2011, that the DEA formally requested the DOD to fund the Global Discovery program. In January 2011, the DOD's DASD CN&GT office responded, in a letter to DEA's Chief of Operations, with its intent to fund the program. A DEA official we spoke with stated that he did not know why the official request for funding occurred after the DOD had already expended more than $26.8 million on the program. The DOD continued to spend money on the Global Discovery program in FY 2011 and, by the end of that fiscal year, had expended a total of approximately $38.7 million, even though the DEA's aircraft was not transferred to the DOD's possession until March 2012.

Moreover, when the DEA did transfer the ATR 500, its second most expensive aircraft, to the DOD's subcontractor, Summit Aviation, for the agreed upon modifications, the DEA did not request any formal documentation of the transfer. Such documentation would typically have included the specific date and time it was transferred, by whom, when it was received by Summit Aviation, and who at Summit Aviation took possession of the aircraft. We were only able to determine the timeframe of the transfer based on a DEA pilot's mission report, which reflects that the aircraft was moved to Summit Aviation in March 2012.

Similarly, the DEA also failed to document its agreement with the DOD, through the DOD's contractor and subcontractor, to perform major modifications to one of the DEA's high-dollar assets. We found no documentation setting forth the parameters of the modifications, such as an MOU or formalized agreement, that detailed when the modifications would be made and completed and what remedy would be provided if the DEA's aircraft was damaged during modification. Therefore, we recommend that the DEA ensure that major agreements involving the transfer or modification of high-dollar assets, such as aircraft, be sufficiently documented to provide a record of the transfer; the terms and conditions related to any agreements pertaining to the assets that are being transferred and any modifications that are to be completed, as well as the responsibility and time frame therefor; and remedial provisions to protect the interests of the DEA in the event of loss or damage that may occur to DEA's assets during that process.

We reviewed DEA flight logs and mission reports to determine if the ATR 500 was flown in Afghanistan prior to March 2012.[13] As described in Table 4, we found that the ATR 500 flew 227 missions both domestically and internationally, although none of the flight logs or mission reports indicated that the aircraft was flown to or conducted any missions in Afghanistan. We determined that between October 2008 and March 2012 the ATR 500 flew transport and extradition missions to Colombia, Guatemala, Grand Cayman, Panama, Ecuador, and Mexico.

We reviewed DEA flight logs and mission reports to determine if the ATR 500 was flown in Afghanistan prior to March 2012.[14] As described in Table 4, we found that the ATR 500 flew 227 missions both domestically and internationally, although none of the flight logs or mission reports indicated that the aircraft was flown to or conducted any missions in Afghanistan. We determined that between October 2008 and March 2012 the ATR 500 flew transport and extradition missions to Colombia, Guatemala, Grand Cayman, Panama, Ecuador, and Mexico.

Table 4

**ATR 500 Missions Flown
Between October 2008 and March 2012**

Date	DEA Support Provided	Purpose of Flight Missions	Missions Flown
10/01/08 – 09/31/10	Flight Logs	Transport personnel; evidence; equipment; and prisoners.	119
10/01/10 – 03/19/12	Mission Reports		108
		Total	**227**

Source: DEA

In September 2012, the DOD awarded a contract for $1,935,506 for a replacement hangar to be built for the DEA at Camp Alvarado, located at the Kabul International Airport, with completion in early calendar year 2013.[15] A DEA official explained to us that the replacement hangar was larger and gave the DEA the ability to house the ATR 500, which was undergoing modifications that had been scheduled for completion by December 2012. However, the modifications to the ATR 500 were not completed on time and the hangar has never housed the DEA's ATR 500 as intended. Instead, the DEA utilized the replacement hangar to house the DEA's two Beech King Air 350's stationed in Afghanistan. Since the DEA's removal of all aviation personnel and assets in Afghanistan in July 2015, the hangar has been utilized by the U.S. Embassy in Kabul and the State Department's Bureau of International Narcotics and Law Enforcement Affairs Office of Aviation (INL Air Wing).

---

[13] A flight log is a record of all the flights an aircraft has flown and it is maintained in the cockpit of each of the DEA's aircraft.

[14] A flight log is a record of all the flights an aircraft has flown and it is maintained in the cockpit of each of the DEA's aircraft.

[15] A DEA official provided the DOD's form 1354, which documented the transfer and acceptance of the DOD's Kabul International Airport Camp Alvarado hangar to the DEA, which the DEA took possession of on November 27, 2013.

In January 2013, the DASD CN&GT's office terminated NSWC Crane as the program office managing the Global Discovery program. A DOD official stated that the DASD CN&GT's office was not satisfied with the progress NSWC Crane had made on the Global Discovery program and because the program had missed its initial delivery date of December 2012, it doubted NSWC Crane's ability to complete the modifications to the ATR 500 in a timely manner. In addition to NSWC Crane's missed delivery date, a DOD official expressed concerns with the selected prime and subcontractors' capabilities, and the overall difficulty of modifying a used transport aircraft with advanced surveillance technologies.[16]

In March 2013, the DEA received, through an MOU with DOD, $8,745,137 to purchase parts for the ATR 500. As of February 2015, the DEA had expended $8,467,591 (97 percent) of those funds. We judgmentally selected three of the seven highest dollar-value expenditures for review, totaling $7,418,932 (88 percent), and found that the expenditures were allowable, supported, and in accordance with the terms and conditions of the MOUs. The majority of the funds, approximately $5 million, were used to purchase two spare engines. We found that the DEA also purchased computer systems and various other parts for the ATR 500.

We asked a DEA official why the spare engines were purchased for the Global Discovery aircraft even though the modifications were not yet completed and the ATR 500 was not operational. The DEA official informed us that the engines were purchased based on the DOD's second anticipated delivery date of December 2013 for the Global Discovery program. In addition, based on the terms and conditions of the MOU, the DEA was required to obligate the DOD funding to purchase parts for the ATR 500 by August 2013 or promptly return the funding. During our fieldwork, we observed the engines, computer systems, and other various parts purchased for the ATR 500 in storage at the DEA's Aviation Operations Center, in Fort Worth, Texas. DEA officials told us that the engines, computer systems, and the majority of parts purchased are specific to an ATR 500 and cannot be utilized on an aircraft other than an ATR 500. Since the DEA does not have another ATR 500 in its fleet, the DEA is unable to utilize these parts until the ATR 500 modification is complete, the aircraft is certified by the FAA as being air-worthy, and the aircraft is returned to the DEA. Therefore, we recommend that the DEA ensure that the parts for the ATR 500 are utilized or returned to the DOD.

Additional changes to the management staff of the Global Discovery program were made by the DOD in February 2013 when Army Research Laboratories (ARL)

---

[16] During our April 21, 2015, visit to Summit Aviation to view the ATR 500, we observed workstations that were built under the DOD's program office, NSWC Crane's supervision, intended for use by DEA Special Agents while conducting surveillance with the ATR 500. A Summit Aviation official showed us the workstations that were made of ship grade metal and weighed 365 pounds each. The DEA had planned to place four workstations in the aircraft. However, the workstations were determined to be too heavy and lighter weight workstations to replace them were built.

became the new program office for the Global Discovery program.[17] In June 2013, Sierra Nevada Corporation (SNC) was awarded the sole source IDIQ for approximately $50 million to complete the Global Discovery program.[18] The first Global Discovery program task order for SNC was signed in July 2013 for $16.6 million.[19] According to both DEA and DOD officials, the estimated delivery date for the ATR 500 was set for December 2013. The DOD's contracting officer for the SNC contract stated that the decision to make the contract sole source was made under the National Security Authority provision of the FAR Part 6.302-6; however the DOD was unable to provide a copy of the sole-source justification to us. SNC awarded subcontracts to Summit Aviation and CTC to complete the modification work on the ATR 500, despite both contractors having already failed to meet the first intended delivery date. SNC officials told us that because the ATR 500 was already housed at Summit Aviation and SNC believed that Summit Aviation could complete the modification by the December 2013 deadline, the subcontract with them was maintained.

Table 5

**DOD's Funding for Global Discovery Program
ATR 500 Modifications**

Fiscal Year (Funds Budgeted)	DOD Program Office	Obligated	Expended	Cumulative Expended
2010	NSWC Crane	$27,227,452	$26,840,076	$26,840,076
2011	NSWC Crane	$12,065,592	$11,825,071	$38,665,147
2012	NSWC Crane	$5,489,531	$5,489,531	$44,154,678
2013	ARL[a]	$18,372,000	$18,365,049	$62,519,727
2014	ARL[a]	$9,485,246	$3,478,515	$65,998,242
Total		**$72,639,821**	**$65,998,242**	

[a] According to a DOD official, although ARL was the DOD program office overseeing the contract for the Global Discovery program, the technical management of the program was handled by CN&GT and CNTPO for FYs 2013 and 2014, respectively.

Source: DOD

---

[17] After encountering problems with NSWC Crane as the program office for the Global Discovery program, the DASD CN&GT office asked the Air Force's Big Safari program office, which is responsible for sustainment and modification of specialized mission aircraft, to take over the Global Discovery program. DEA and DOD officials stated that Big Safari required that the ATR 500 be restored to its original FAA certified condition before it agreed to take over the Global Discovery program. The restoration included completion of required maintenance and engine repair due to foreign object debris damage. According to a DOD official, a contractor's wrench went through the engine. In January 2013, after the aircraft had been returned to its original flyable condition, a DOD official stated that Big Safari declined to take over the Global Discovery program, apparently based on concerns regarding the state of the program.

[18] IDIQ contracts provide for an indefinite quantity of services for a fixed time. The base contract is not funded until a task order is issued and the government is only accountable for the amount of the task order. The Global Discovery program was one of several in this particular SNC IDIQ contract.

[19] SNC received $18,372,000 for the Global Discovery program through four DOD military interdepartmental purchase requests.

By the end of FY 2013, more than $62.5 million had been expended on the ATR 500's modifications, which was almost triple the original estimated amount of $22 million to purchase and modify the Global Discovery aircraft. In addition, the ATR 500 did not receive all of the originally intended modifications. Specifically, DEA officials stated the DOD's Program Manager decided to permanently mount the optical cameras to the aircraft in order to reduce technical risks, speed up the modification timeline, and to reduce costs. According to a DOD official, in October 2013 the DASD CN&GT office was unsatisfied with the progress of the Global Discovery program, the Program Manager was removed, and a new Program Manager from CNTPO was appointed. The DEA was concerned about having the large cameras fix-mounted because it would be evident to anyone looking at the aircraft that this was a surveillance aircraft, which the DEA believed would prevent their ability to fly through countries as easily as if the cameras retracted up into the aircraft as originally planned.[20] The DEA Aviation Division's Special Agent in Charge and two DEA Assistant Special Agents in Charge met with the new DOD Global Discovery Program Manager to discuss the fix-mounting of the cameras. Both the DEA and DOD ultimately agreed that the cameras would be mounted to the aircraft with the option of manually removing and storing them in the ATR 500 when not needed. See Figure 2.

Figure 2

**Fix-Mounted MX-20 Cameras
on the DEA's ATR 500**

Source: DEA

In December 2013, the Global Discovery program missed its second intended delivery date. The DEA Aviation Division official overseeing the Global Discovery program stated that he expressed his concerns to the DOD about continuing to pay the same entities who failed to meet the first deadline and whose technical capabilities had come into question. In response to the DEA's concerns, CTC's

---

[20] According to DOD and DEA personnel, many countries will not allow aircraft with surveillance capabilities to fly through their airspace.

subcontract was terminated in January 2014. A SNC official told the OIG that it took this action because it had determined CTC did not have the capability to complete the work.

In April 2014, an FAA representative responsible for certifying the aircraft's flightworthiness observed oblong holes in the aircraft's frame. These oblong holes were found when splice plates had to be removed from the ATR 500 so Summit Aviation could install fabricated frame doublers that would be used to strengthen sections of the aircraft frame at the locations where the MX-20 cameras would be mounted. Removing the splice plates required that a technician drill through the rivets that connected the splice plates to the aircraft frame. After the splice plates were removed, the oblong holes were discovered. While Summit Aviation asserted that the oblong holes were already in the aircraft prior to its work, the situation was further impacted by the fact that Summit Aviation had drilled oblong holes in the frame doublers to match the oblong holes in the aircraft frame. According to a DEA Aviation Division official, he was surprised that the Summit Aviation technician drilled oblong holes in the doublers because it is common knowledge that rivets cannot be effectively placed in oblong holes and the strength of the rivet is dependent upon a 360 degree circular hole for contact, which an oblong hole could never provide. The ATR 500 was rendered un-flyable as a result of these improper modifications, and the estimated cost to correct the problem and meet the FAA certification requirement was an additional $6 million.

According to DOD's Program Manager, in August 2014 a progress meeting was held with SNC. After this meeting, the Program Manager expressed concerns that the contractors were providing incomplete and inaccurate technical and financial data that lacked consistency and traceability. The Program Manager also expressed doubt that the DOD's contractor could complete the modification and said that the Global Discovery program needed to be shut down. During this time, the Global Discovery program's intended delivery date of March 2014 slid to July 2014, and then to September 2014.

Figure 3

Oblong Holes of the DEA's ATR 500

 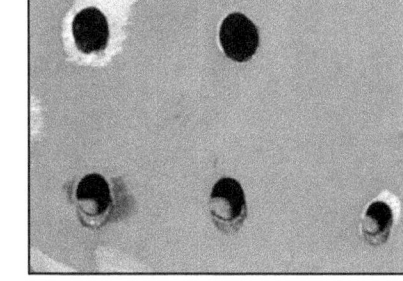

Source: DOD

According to SNC and Summit Aviation officials, Summit Aviation stopped work on the ATR 500 in October 2014 because SNC's funding had run out.[21] DOD officials informed us that the DASD CN&GT office considered ending the Global Discovery program without completing the modification of the ATR 500 because the cost to repair the frame was estimated at $6 million and, according to DOD officials; the value of the aircraft at that time was only $6 million. Had the determination to end the program been made, the ATR 500 would either have been scrapped or been brought back to flying condition at some expense and returned to the DEA without completing the modifications. A DEA Aviation Division official stated that the DEA was uncertain if the Global Discovery program could be completed and requested that the ATR 500 be returned to the DEA. Ultimately, the DOD decided to commit more funding to complete the Global Discovery program.

In March 2015, the DOD signed a firm-fixed-price contract with SNC for an additional $8,539,642 to repair the aircraft, complete the modification, and deliver a flyable aircraft in June 2016. However, as of January 2016, the plane remains at a Summit Aviation facility even though Summit Aviation has no subcontract to complete the work. A Summit Aviation official told the OIG that Summit Aviation is working on the ATR 500's modification on a time and material basis until a subcontract with SNC has been signed. Further, a DEA Aviation Division official explained to the OIG that additional originally agreed upon modifications will not be made to the ATR 500. For example the radar system, for which the DOD obligated approximately $1.5 million, will not be installed.[22] The DASD CN&GT office is working to provide the radar system itself to the DEA upon completion of the other ATR 500 modifications. According to a DEA official, the estimated additional cost for the DEA to install the radar system is $3 million.

---

[21] As of September 2014, SNC had received $16,562,486 from the DOD and requested additional funding to complete the Global Discovery program.

[22] The planned radar system can detect and monitor compact vehicles traveling at speeds between 5 and 50 miles per hour and automatically track vehicles or people.

Figure 4

Global Discovery Program Intended Delivery Dates Missed

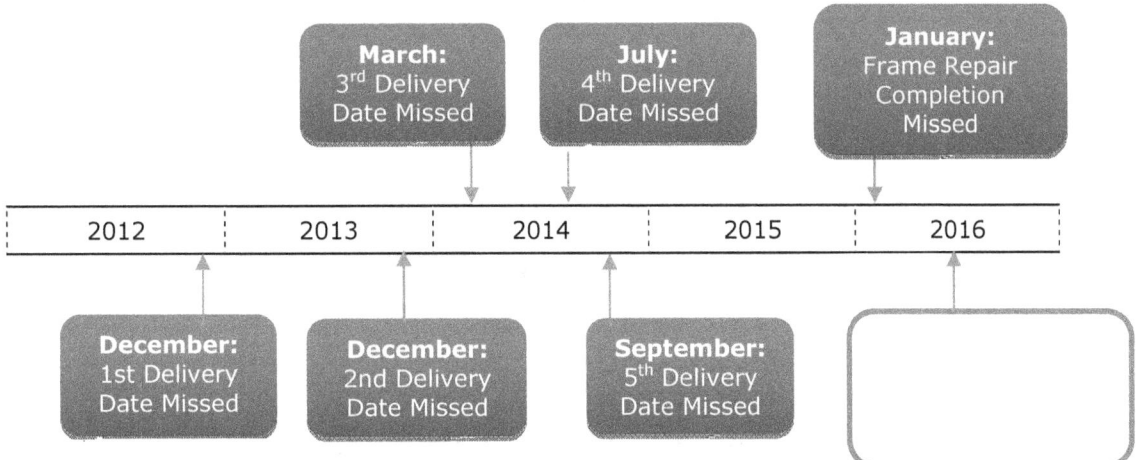

a The timeline of missed Global Discovery program intended delivery dates includes contractor projected completion dates.

Source: DEA and DOD

In total, the DEA and the DOD have spent more than $86 million on the Global Discovery program. As of March 2016, the ATR 500 still sits un-flyable at Summit Aviation's facility and yet another delivery date of June 2016 has been established. More than 7 years after the DEA's major purchase of an aircraft to conduct surveillance and counternarcotics missions in Afghanistan, the ATR 500 modifications remain ongoing, and the aircraft has never flown in Afghanistan where a hangar, specifically built to house the aircraft, has stood since 2013. In the meantime, the DEA has removed all aviation assets and ceased operations in Afghanistan, so it is unlikely the plane will ever fly there.[23]

DEA's MOUs with the DOD

The DEA entered into four additional MOUs with the DOD to support the DEA's aviation operations in Afghanistan, for a total of $20,335,000 between FYs 2012 and 2015. The MOUs were intended to support the DEA's two Beech King Air 350s operating in Afghanistan until the deployment of the Global Discovery ATR 500. According to the terms of the MOUs, funds were to be expended on: (1) the DEA's contractor, L-3, to support operations and maintenance for two Beech King Air 350 aircraft in Afghanistan; (2) landing fees for DEA's aircraft in Afghanistan; (3) electricity and generator maintenance at Camp Alvarado in Afghanistan; (4) temporary duty costs (TDY) for DEA's aviation detachment in Afghanistan; and (5) flares for the ALE-47 Airborne Countermeasures Dispenser System. We reviewed the DEA's MOUs with the DOD to determine if the

---

23 A DEA official stated that once completed, the DEA plans to utilize the ATR 500 for operations in the Caribbean, Central America, and South America, though that was not, of course, the purpose of the funding or the Global Discovery program.

whistleblower allegation – that the DEA had misused DOD funding by misdirecting, diverting, and spending it for purposes unrelated to supporting the DEA's two aircraft operating in Afghanistan – had any indications of merit.

Figure 5

DEA's Beech King Air 350

Source: DEA

MOU Transaction Testing

As of February 2015, the DEA had expended $13,330,447 (66 percent) of the total MOU funds received from the DOD for these purposes. We judgmentally selected a sample of 91 expenditures, totaling $8,000,964 (60 percent) to determine if costs charged to the MOUs were allowable, properly authorized, adequately supported, and in compliance with the terms and conditions.[24] All 91 of the transactions we tested included non-personnel expenditures while 28 also contained personnel expenditures. We discuss the results of our testing below.

Non-Personnel Costs Charged to the MOUs

Our sample included non-personnel expenditures in the amount of $6,810,003. Specifically, we reviewed expenditures related to the operation and maintenance of the DEA's aircraft stationed in Afghanistan, TDY costs for contractors' travel expenses to and from Afghanistan, and training. The DEA also paid for electricity and generator maintenance at Camp Alvarado in Kabul, Afghanistan. To determine if costs were allowable, properly authorized, adequately supported, and in compliance with the MOUs' terms and conditions we reviewed supporting documentation including contractor billings, purchase orders, invoices, and receipts.

---

[24] $7,218,735 of the 91 expenditures we tested pertained to the DEA's contractor, L-3.

20

<u>Unallowable Non-Personnel Expenditures</u>

The MOUs required the DEA to use, "...the funding provided...for supporting the flight operations of DEA Aviation in Afghanistan." Based on our testing, we found $671,041 in unallowable non-personnel expenditures charged to the MOUs as described in Table 6.

Table 6

Unallowable Non-Personnel Expenditures Charged to the MOUs

Expenditure	Unallowable Use	Questioned Cost
Maintenance of Aircraft not in Afghanistan	Non-Afghanistan operations	$602,196
Training (including travel to training)	Training for DEA and L-3 employees that did not go to Afghanistan	$32,211
Camp Alvarado Generator Fuel and Service in 2011	Expenditures outside the MOU period of performance	$20,247
Missions in Haiti, the Bahamas, Peru, and Florida	Non-Afghanistan missions	$8,122
Duplicate Expenditures (travel-related and generator service in Kabul)	Duplicate charges	$6,776
Other (satellite phone service, room cleaning, Fed Ex charges, travel for L-3 employee unrelated to DEA's Aviation Program)	Non-Afghanistan operations	$1,489
	Total	**$671,041**

Source: OIG

L-3 had billed the DEA, and the DEA's Contracting Officer (CO) approved $602,196 in unallowable costs for the maintenance of one aircraft that never flew in Afghanistan and two more aircraft that were assigned and operating missions for the DEA out of Fort Lauderdale, Florida. A DEA official stated that the aircraft that never flew in Afghanistan was used for training pilots at the DEA's Aviation Operations Center in Fort Worth, Texas. For the other two aircraft, we took exception to one because the DEA charged maintenance up to 19 months prior to the aircraft leaving for Afghanistan. The other aircraft was stationed in Fort Lauderdale, Florida 7 months after returning from Afghanistan and the DEA continued to charge the aircraft's maintenance to the MOUs. An Aviation Division official stated that the DEA believed maintenance charges that were incurred prior to and after an aircraft returned from deployment in Afghanistan were allowable expenditures under the MOUs. However, the Aviation Division official also agreed that maintenance costs should not have continued to be charged to the MOU after the aircraft was reassigned to Fort Lauderdale, Florida.

We also found $8,122 in unallowable travel expenditures related to missions in Port Au Prince, Haiti; the Bahamas; Lima, Peru; and Florida – travel that was unrelated to the DEA's aviation operations in Afghanistan. Aviation Division officials agreed that these costs should not have been applied to its DOD MOU expenses. However, as of September 2015, DEA officials had not provided documentation that these unallowable charges were corrected in its accounting records. In addition, we found that $40,476 was spent on non-Afghanistan related operations, duplicate expenditures, and training for DEA and L-3 personnel who never traveled to

Afghanistan for DEA aviation operations purposes. We also determined that $20,247 was expended outside of the MOU period of performance. Therefore, we question the $671,041 in unallowable non-personnel expenditures charged to the MOUs. The DEA agreed with our $20,247 in question costs for expenditures outside of the MOU period of performance and with $2,060 in question costs for duplicate charges incurred by the Kabul Country Office for paying the State Department for the same invoice twice.

Unsupported Non-Personnel Expenditures

Based on our testing, we also found $78,208 in potentially allowable, but unsupported non-personnel expenditures charged to the MOUs as described in Table 7.

Table 7

**Unsupported Non-Personnel
Expenditures Charged to the MOUs**

Expenditure	Question Cost
Camp Alvarado Electricity and Generator Service	$51,946
Training	$12,875
Maintenance of Aircraft	$12,366
Travel	$950
Other (Communications)	$71
Total	**$78,208**

Source: OIG

The DEA obligated a portion of the MOU funds to the DEA's Kabul Country Office for electricity and generator maintenance at Camp Alvarado in Kabul, Afghanistan. For all purchases made in a foreign country the State Department is required to contract for and make purchases on the DEA's behalf. In return, the DEA reimburses the State Department for the goods and services that were purchased. According to the DEA's policy issued in September 2014, the DEA's foreign offices are required to scan and attach obligation and payment support documentation in the DEA's Unified Financial Management System (UFMS) for goods and services procured by the State Department on behalf of the DEA. The DEA's policy before September 2014 required obligation and payment support documentation to be maintained in hardcopy. We found four transactions totaling $51,946 that were charged to the MOUs but that lacked adequate supporting documentation. Specifically, the DEA either did not maintain adequate supporting documents at the Kabul Country Office or the documentation that the DEA provided to us was illegible. In addition, the Kabul Country Office had to request copies of supporting documentation from the State Department for 17 of the 52 expenditures we tested because the Kabul Country Office had not maintained supporting documentation in UFMS or in hardcopy form. Because the DEA did not always properly maintain adequate supporting documentation, the DEA is unable to verify that it paid for products or services related to DEA aviation operations. The DEA agreed with our $51,946 in question costs for unsupported electricity and generator services at Camp Alvarado in Kabul, Afghanistan. We recommend that the DEA ensure that the Kabul Country Office follows the DEA's policy for maintaining obligation and payment support documentation in UFMS to ensure the goods and services charged from other agencies are accurate, supported, and allowable.

According to the DEA's Aviation Operations Handbook, Section 6, Training and Standardization, the Aviation Training Officer is responsible for maintaining training records in sufficient detail to ensure compliance and to provide effective program management. The DEA paid a total of $84,730 for 59 required training courses for pilots and mechanics to deploy overseas. However, the DEA was unable to provide certificates of completion to certify that individuals had, in fact, completed the training and when it was completed.[25] After the conclusion of our audit fieldwork, the DEA was able to provide evidence of country clearances that the DEA stated can only be issued after required training courses are completed. Based on our review of the DEA's documentation, $12,875 for 27 required training courses remain unsupported. The DEA's policies for both DEA and contract personnel require the Aviation Division to maintain proper training records in order to document that trainings were attended and completed. Without such records the DEA cannot verify that its personnel received the requisite training to carry out their duties or support the expenses it paid for employees to attend these training courses. We recommend that the DEA establish procedures to ensure the Aviation Division adheres to its policy requiring that training records be maintained in sufficient detail for both the DEA and contract personnel. In addition, we found $13,387 for aircraft maintenance, travel, and other non-personnel costs that could not be supported. In total, we question $78,208 in unsupported non-personnel expenditures that were charged to the MOUs and recommend that the DEA remedy this cost.

Personnel Costs Charged to the MOUs

Of the 91 selected expenditures, 28 included personnel costs totaling $3,683,170. We judgmentally selected 10 of the 28 personnel-related expenditures, totaling $1,190,961 for review. Personnel costs consisted of payments to contract pilots and mechanics to support the DEA's aviation operations in Afghanistan. We reviewed $720,508 in direct labor and $470,453 in special pay charged to the MOUs.[26] All personnel costs charged to the MOUs between 2012 and 2014 were billed by L-3 to the DEA through its aviation contract. The DEA's aviation contract with L-3 established the approved hourly rates for contract pilots and mechanics including special pay rates in Afghanistan. The contract also specified the approved rates that L-3 was allowed to charge for overhead, general and administrative fees, and other fees in relation to personnel costs. To determine

---

[25] In addition, the DEA's aviation contract states that the contractor (L-3) should provide documented training records for each individual attending a training course to the Contracting Officer's Technical Representative (COTR), or authorized representative, within 5 working days. However, we found that 18 of the 59 trainings that did not have a completion certificate were trainings for L-3 contract personnel.

[26] A contractor's special pay is in addition to regular hourly wages and includes hazard, hardship, cost of living adjustments, retention bonuses, and shelter pay.

if costs were allowable, properly authorized, adequately supported, and in compliance with MOU terms and conditions, we reviewed supporting documentation including contractor billings, L-3's payroll report, and timecards.

Lack of Internal Controls

We obtained L-3 monthly invoices, from the DEA for 9 months between FYs 2012 and 2014, which we selected for review of personnel costs, totaling $1,190,961. At the time of our review, the DEA received a monthly summary invoice from L-3, which simply included the contractor's name and the total personnel hours billed. An Aviation Division official stated that only L-3's summary of monthly invoices were reviewed by Aviation Division personnel prior to payment and that the DEA did not perform any reconciliation to or verification of supporting documentation for L-3's payroll charges. Therefore, we obtained from L-3 supporting documentation such as payroll reports, approved timecards, and other payroll supporting documentation for labor and special pay charges billed to the DEA.[27] When we compared L-3's supporting documentation to its summary monthly invoices and the hours billed, we determined that the hours billed were not reflective of the actual hours worked within that month. Of the 217 direct labor and 331 special pay expenditures L-3 billed to the DEA for the 9 months we reviewed, initially 133 (61 percent) direct labor and 90 (27 percent) special pay expenditures could not be reconciled to L-3's payroll reports, approved timecards, and other payroll supporting documentation provided by L-3. This occurred because L-3 did not adhere to its payroll calendar when charging the DEA for contract employees' labor and did not list the actual pay dates on its summary invoices. Therefore, the summary invoices could not be reconciled to the payroll reports generated based on L-3's payroll calendar. After more than 5 months of repeated follow-up by the OIG, L-3 provided documentation and explanation to support the majority of direct labor expenditures. However, as of January 2016, L-3 has not responded to 84 of the 90 special pay expenditures that could not be reconciled.

Based on our analysis, we determined that the DEA's Aviation Division does not have adequate policies or procedures for receiving, reviewing, and paying contractor invoices for personnel costs. Specifically, there is no requirement for the DEA's CO or COTR to review supporting documentation, such as payroll reports, approved timecards, and other supporting documentation, prior to contract personnel being paid. We also determined that the DEA's current aviation contract with L-3 does not even specify what supporting documentation is required to be provided to the DEA for contractor personnel expenditures. Without adequate internal controls, the Aviation Division cannot determine if the personnel expenditures being claimed are accurate before payment. Therefore, we recommend that the DEA strengthen its internal controls by establishing procedures on how it oversees and verifies the Aviation Division's contractor's performance, to ensure that contractors provide adequate support for the charges that are billed to

---

[27] During our review of L-3's supporting documentation, we determined that L-3 did not follow its policy requiring that employees who do not have access to L-3's automated payroll system complete and sign their individual timecard attesting to the accuracy of hours worked.

the DEA and that the DEA review supporting documentation prior to paying summary monthly invoices.

Unallowable Personnel Expenditures

Based on our testing of direct labor and special pay expenditures for the 9 months we reviewed, we found $47,453 in unallowable personnel expenditures charged to the MOUs. Specifically, we determined that the DEA approved and paid overbillings made by L-3 for $12,432 in direct labor charges and $35,021 in special pay. Therefore, we recommend that the DEA remedy the $47,453 in unallowable personnel expenditures charged to the MOUs.

Overhead and G&A Fees for Personnel Costs

In its contract with the DEA for aviation support, L-3 charged overhead and general and administrative (G&A) fees. The rates for these fees were approved by the Defense Contract Management Agency. L-3 applied overhead and G&A fees to direct costs when applicable. We reviewed overhead and G&A fees charged to the 9 months of personnel expenditures we selected in our sample and determined the overhead and G&A fees L-3 charged were accurate and supported.[28]

Additional Costs Associated with the Global Discovery Program

According to each of the four MOUs that the DEA entered into with the DOD between FYs 2012 and 2015, the DEA was required to use the funding provided to support the operation and maintenance of the DEA's two Beech King Air 350 airplanes until the deployment of the ATR 500 (Global Discovery aircraft) based at the Kabul Airport in support of the Government of Afghanistan. Specifically, the MOUs stated that the funding will provide for flight crews, ground support, and associated maintenance services necessary to support aviation operations in Afghanistan. We found that between FYs 2012 and 2014, the DEA spent $1,664,699 of DOD MOU funding intended for aviation operations in Afghanistan on maintenance for the Global Discovery program's ATR 500, pilot and mechanic training for the ATR 500, and travel to the DOD's subcontractor, Summit Aviation, to observe the program's progress. The following table shows the unallowable amount of the Global Discovery program expenditures charged to the MOUs.

---

[28] We did not review the method by which the fee rates L-3 charged were determined. However, we did determine that all fee rates L-3 charged were approved by the DEA.

Table 8

**Unallowable Global Discovery Program
Expenditures Charged to the MOUs**

Expenditure	Question Cost
ATR 500 Maintenance	$1,411,611
Pilot, Mechanic, and Support Staff Training	$207,218
Travel	$45,870
Total	**$1,664,699**

Source: DEA

We found $1,411,611 in unallowable ATR 500 maintenance-related expenditures charged to the MOUs. When we visited Summit Aviation's facility in Delaware where the ATR 500 was being modified, we interviewed Summit Aviation personnel and learned that Summit Aviation performed routine maintenance on the ATR 500 in addition to the modification work that was underway. Specifically, after transporting the aircraft to Summit Aviation's facility, the DEA paid Summit Aviation and other companies through its contract with L-3, $1,411,611 to maintain the ATR 500, with funds intended for aviation operations in Afghanistan.

- In January 2015, L-3 paid Summit Aviation $847,971 for (1) annual checks; (2) aircraft re-certifications; (3) overhaul and inspections; and (4) parts replacement on the ATR 500.

- L-3 also paid Summit Aviation $252,609 in February 2013 to remove the ATR 500's existing engines in preparation for Pratt & Whitney Engine Services, Inc. to perform inspection and overhaul service on them, for which the DEA paid $311,031.

L-3 informed us that their existing purchase order still had a balance of $262,102 available for Summit Aviation's services. In total, the DEA paid $1,411,611 through L-3 to maintain the ATR 500 while in the DOD's possession and while it was undergoing major modifications. While we believe it was not unreasonable to maintain this aircraft during that period, it was unallowable for the DEA to divert approximately $1.4 million in routine maintenance-related expenditures for the ATR 500 from the MOUs intended to support on-going operations in Afghanistan when, of course, the ATR 500 was not ready and has never flown in Afghanistan.

We also found $207,218 in additional unallowable training-related expenditures charged to the MOUs, which included:

- $40,008 to train three L-3 mechanics in October 2014 to maintain the ATR 500 aircraft.

- $161,429 for pilot training costs, which included:

  o $83,151 to train DEA pilots for the ATR 500 and to deploy to Afghanistan.

- $49,376 for one L-3 pilot to attend ATR training classes; temporary duty assignment charges for more than 5 months at the DEA's Aviation Operations Center, and to provide mission support on DEA's ATR 320 in St. Croix, Panama City, Bogota, and other locations. The mission support was intended to allow the L-3 pilot to obtain ATR flight hours.
- $28,902 to hire and train another L-3 pilot for the ATR 500, who actually was terminated due to poor performance at the end of training.

- $5,781 to train ATR 500 support staff to deploy to Afghanistan.

A DEA official stated that the L-3 mechanics were trained to work on the ATR 500 because the DEA expected to utilize the aircraft shortly after its anticipated modification delivery date of December 2013. The DEA official also informed us that DEA Special Agent pilots and L-3 pilots were scheduled to conduct test flights on the ATR 500 beginning in August 2014. In order to meet DOD's flight test schedule for the ATR 500, almost all of the DEA's pilots that were trained on the ATR 320 needed to be appropriately trained before they could operate the ATR 500.[29] However, as discussed above, these MOUs were intended to pay for ongoing operations with the Beech King Air 350s prior to the deployment of the ATR 500, which was not flyable as of March 2016 and did not, at any time, operate in Afghanistan as originally intended. Therefore, these expenditures related to the ATR 500 were unallowable.

As a primary stakeholder in the Global Discovery program, the DEA visited the DOD's subcontractor's space multiple times throughout the program. To view the progress that was being made on the ATR 500's modification, the DEA sent the Aviation Division's Assistant Special Agent in Charge, Quality Assurance Specialist, and other personnel to SNC and Summit Aviation's facilities.[30] We reviewed 33 travel vouchers for Aviation Division personnel traveling between August 2012 and August 2014 at a cost of $44,559. We found that the Aviation Division's Special Agent in Charge traveled to DEA headquarters for a meeting pertaining to the Global Discovery program at a cost of $1,311. In total, the DEA spent $45,870 in MOU funds intended for aviation operations in Afghanistan on trips pertaining to the Global Discovery program's progress. DEA officials stated that they believed it was important to observe DOD's contractor's progress on the aircraft, express issues concerning work being conducted by the contractors to DOD officials, and to help ensure the completion of the aircraft. We agree that the DEA's travel was necessary to assist the DOD in overseeing the modifications being made to the DEA's ATR 500. However, based on the terms and conditions of the MOUs, funding was intended to pay for on-going aviation operations in Afghanistan and the ATR 500 did not at any time operate in Afghanistan.

---

[29] Prior to purchasing the ATR 500 in September 2008 for the Global Discovery program, the DEA had in its fleet an ATR 320 aircraft, which according to Aviation Division officials has similar pilot and mechanic training requirements to the ATR 500.

[30] SNC has been the DOD's prime contractor for the Global Discovery program since June 2013 and the DEA's ATR 500 has been housed at Summit Aviation's (SNC's subcontractor) facility since March 2012.

In total, we question $2,461,401 in unallowable and unsupported expenditures charged to the MOUs. We also recommend that the DEA put the $262,102 of MOU funds intended for ATR 500 maintenance to a better use.

MOU Requirements

Upon agreeing to the MOUs that it signed with the DOD, the DEA agreed to: (1) properly commit and obligate funds received according to the terms and conditions of the MOUs; (2) maintain full and complete records and accounts with respect to the use of funds in accordance with generally accepted accounting principles; and (3) ensure that expenditures conform to the MOU requirements. To determine if the DEA met those requirements, we reviewed how quickly the DEA obligated MOU funds or returned unused funds to the DOD. We also reviewed monthly, quarterly, and final programmatic and financial reports that the DEA was required to submit to the DOD in order to determine the reports' accuracy and whether they were submitted in a timely manner.[31]

Untimely Remittance of DOD Funding

Pursuant to the terms of the MOUs, the DEA was required to obligate funds by September 30th, and to return any unobligated funds to the DOD before the end of the fiscal year. Shortly after we began our audit in November 2014, we determined that the DEA had not returned unobligated funds in a timely manner. In fact, it was only after we began making inquiries into this matter that the DEA returned some unobligated funds to the DOD. The following table shows the amounts and dates for all of the unobligated funds that the DEA returned to the DOD during the period of our review.

Table 9

Return of Unused Funds after Fiscal Year

MOU FY	Due By	Date Returned	Late (Months)	Amount
2012	09/30/12	02/12/15	28	$28,658
2013	09/30/13	01/14/15	15	$84,474
2014	09/30/14	01/14/15	3	$40,000
			Total	**$153,132**

Source: DEA and DOD

Financial and Programmatic Reports Provided to the DOD

According to the DOD's Military Interdepartmental Purchase Requests (MIPRs), associated with the FYs 2013 and 2014 MOUs, the DEA is required to submit monthly financial reports to the DOD including goods and services purchased with MOU funds, according to the cost categories established in the MOUs. We compared the DEA's general ledger for the MOUs with the monthly

---

[31] The monthly financial reports were not evaluated for timeliness because the DOD did not require a due date for those reports.

28

information on 27 of 51 monthly reports that it submitted to the DOD. As a result, we found that the information the DEA provided to the DOD on the goods and services it purchased was accurate.

Similarly, the MOUs required the DEA to submit quarterly reports to the DOD for goods and services purchased, including accounting or audit information, within 30 days of the end of each quarter. However, while the DEA was already providing financial information on a monthly basis, the DOD asked the DEA to provide quarterly programmatic reports. The quarterly programmatic reports included the total number of missions flown, number of mission declined, and the availability of aircraft including downtime for maintenance. Of the three MOUs the DEA received between FYs 2012 and 2014, we reviewed all quarterly reports for each MOU and found that, with the exception of one report that was submitted 29 days late, the reports were filed on time. We discuss in more detail the accuracy of the DEA's programmatic reports that it submitted to the DOD in the *Aviation Operations in Afghanistan* section of this report.

The MOUs also required that the DEA submit a final accounting report following the end of each fiscal year, but no later than November 15. We determined that the DEA did not submit final accounting reports to the DOD for all four MOUs we reviewed. When we asked DEA officials about the final accounting reports, they stated that although the period for obligating MOU funds was one fiscal year, the DOD's FY 2012 and 2013 MIPRs stated the period of accomplishing the requirements of the MOUs was from October 1 and continued until services were completed.[32] A DEA official also added that a final accounting report could not be provided by November 15 because outstanding services were not yet recorded in the accounting records. While DEA's reasoning appears acceptable, we believe that if it was unable to meet the terms of the MOUs in this regard, the DEA should have worked with the DOD on establishing a suitable date before it entered into any additional MOUs with the DOD. Therefore, we recommend that the DEA ensure the MOUs it enters into with the DOD have suitable dates for all required financial reporting.

Aviation Operations in Afghanistan

As previously noted, the purpose of four of the MOUs was to provide assistance to the DEA's aviation operations in Afghanistan. However, we found that the MOUs did not contain goals, objectives, or any other measurable performance metrics to determine if the DEA's use of MOU funds had any impact on its

---

[32] We determined the FY 2014 MOU period of performance was October 1, 2013, until September 30, 2014.

counternarcotics mission in Afghanistan.[33] In the absence of any prescribed performance measurements, we reviewed the DEA's quarterly reports submitted to the DOD and the DEA's mission reports to determine the number of missions flown, mission requests declined, and the availability of aircraft including downtime for maintenance.

Missions Flown and Missions Declined

The DEA operated two Beech King Air 350 aircraft in Afghanistan; one equipped with surveillance capabilities and one predominantly used for transporting personnel and equipment. Between October 2011 and February 2015, we determined that 1,308 missions were flown in Afghanistan by DEA aircraft. As illustrated in Figure 6, the majority of the DEA's flights flown (79 percent) were for transporting personnel and equipment.

Figure 6

**DEA's Afghanistan Missions Flown
October 2011 through February 2015**

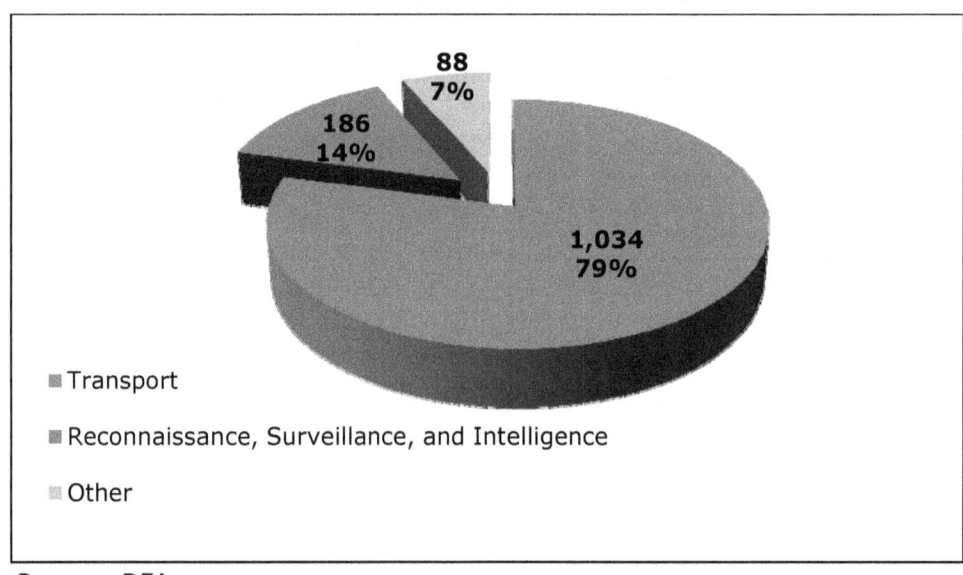

Source: DEA

A DEA official informed us that the majority of mission requests the DEA received in Afghanistan were for transport because it is the safest way to move personnel and equipment in a combat environment. When we asked the DOD Program Manager if the DOD was satisfied with the amount of reconnaissance, surveillance, and intelligence missions (14 percent) that the DEA had conducted in

---

[33] The DOJ OIG's FY 2015 Top Management Challenges states that the Department "must work to develop, collect, and analyze meaningful and outcome-oriented performance metrics." In addition, research indicates that collecting the right data and having clearly defined goals and progress measures can assist agencies in more effectively measuring their efforts. OIG Top Management and Performance Challenges Facing the Department of Justice, https://oig.justice.gov/challenges/2015.pdf (accessed December 8, 2015).

Afghanistan, he stated that he was not completely satisfied and had asked Aviation Division officials to fly more surveillance flights. Between February 2012 and January 2015 the DEA received more than 1,000 mission requests that could not be fulfilled, including 105 requests for reconnaissance, surveillance, and intelligence missions. As shown in Figure 7, over three-quarters of the requested missions were declined by the DEA due to aircraft not being available (57 percent) or the aircraft was undergoing maintenance (19 percent).

Figure 7

**DEA's Afghanistan Mission Requests Declined
February 2012 through January 2015**

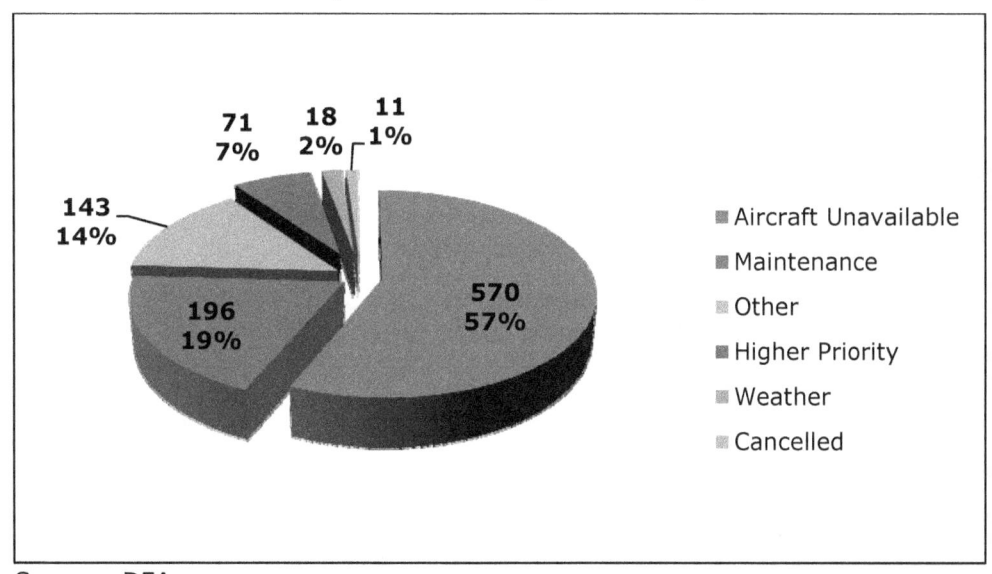

Source: DEA

We learned that when DEA aircraft were unavailable, DEA Special Agents in Afghanistan were able to request mission assistance from the State Department's Bureau of International Narcotics and Law Enforcement Affairs Office of Aviation (INL Air Wing).[34] Between October 2011 and May 2015, at the DEA's request, the State Department flew 1,223 missions for general support such as transport, interdiction, reconnaissance, and training operations for the DEA.[35] A DEA official also stated that the Global Discovery aircraft was expected to assist with the counternarcotics surveillance missions in Afghanistan, thus providing an additional aviation asset to meet mission needs. However, the ATR 500 did not make it to Afghanistan, as detailed above.

---

[34] The State Department's INL Air Wing, commonly known as Embassy Air, oversees a combined fleet of 132 active aircraft and helicopters operating around the world. Between October 2011 and May 2015, the INL Air Wing had on average each fiscal year 8 aircraft and 21 helicopters operating in Afghanistan.

[35] A State Department official informed us that the State Department did not track DEA missions requested and declined.

Aircraft Availability

We also determined that the DEA had difficulty keeping its surveillance aircraft operational in Afghanistan. Between October 2012 and September 2013 the surveillance aircraft was almost completely unavailable due to maintenance issues. During that time period, it only flew 8 reconnaissance, surveillance, or intelligence missions and the DEA reported that 40 additional reconnaissance, surveillance, or intelligence missions were requested but had to be declined. A DEA pilot told us that once Special Agents in Afghanistan knew the surveillance aircraft was unavailable they stopped requesting aviation support for reconnaissance, surveillance, and intelligence missions. Therefore, the need for assistance was likely higher than the reported number of unfilled requests. As shown in Figure 8, between October 2012 and September 2013 when the surveillance aircraft was under maintenance and largely unavailable, the number of missions that were requested but had to be declined fell substantially. Once the surveillance aircraft became available again in October 2013, the number of missions that were requested but had to be declined increased.

Figure 8

**DEA's Surveillance Aircraft in Afghanistan
Between FYs 2011 and 2014**

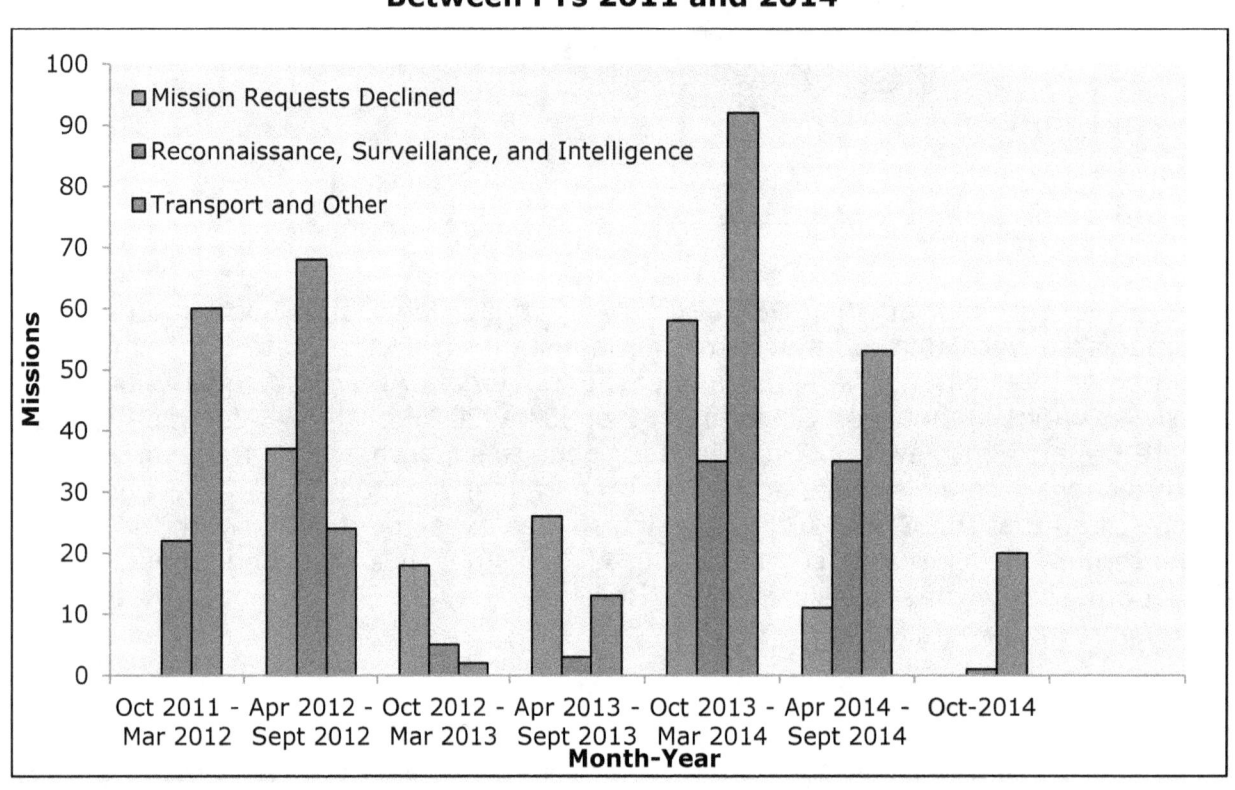

Note: On October 15, 2014, the DEA permanently removed its surveillance aircraft from Afghanistan.

Source: DEA

An Aviation Division official stated that having the necessary parts ready and on-site when the aircraft went down for maintenance in Afghanistan was a challenge. For example, the surveillance aircraft was removed from Afghanistan in October 2012 and brought back to the Aviation Operations Center to receive an updated instrument system and a scheduled inspection. We were also informed that the aircraft had a leaky door needing repair for which the DEA did not have the parts on hand. A DEA official stated that despite these maintenance issues, the Aviation Division assisted in the disruption of nine drug trafficking organizations and the dismantlement of five more organizations in Afghanistan between 2012 and 2013. However, removing the aircraft that was predominantly used to conduct surveillance missions, without providing a substitute aircraft, for approximately 8 months, reflected inadequate planning by the DEA in the management of its aviation assets in Afghanistan. We believe that the DEA should have worked with the DOD to ensure that the DEA's aviation needs to support the counternarcotics effort in Afghanistan were being fully met. Therefore, we recommend that the DEA work with the DOD to establish clear objectives and deliverables, and a method for tracking deliverables to ascertain whether these efforts are achieving the desired objectives.

Accuracy of Programmatic Reports

Although the MOUs did not contain goals, objectives, or performance measurements to determine what impact, if any, the DEA's use of MOU funds had on its counternarcotics mission in Afghanistan, the DOD did require the DEA to submit quarterly programmatic reports on missions flown and missions declined in Afghanistan. In the absence of other performance measurements, we reviewed the programmatic reports that the DEA submitted to the DOD between April 2012 and September 2014. However, as illustrated in Figure 9, we found that the data the DEA submitted to the DOD in these reports was not accurate, and that the extent of the over-reporting or under-reporting of missions flown and requests denied varied significantly over time. For example, we found that for the second quarter of FY 2014, the DEA over-reported its number of missions flown by 46. Therefore, it did not fly 26 percent of the 178 missions it reported for that quarter. In addition, the DEA under-reported the number of mission requests it declined by 70 percent for that same quarter.

Figure 9

**Missions Over or Under-Reported to the DOD
Between FYs 2012 and 2014**

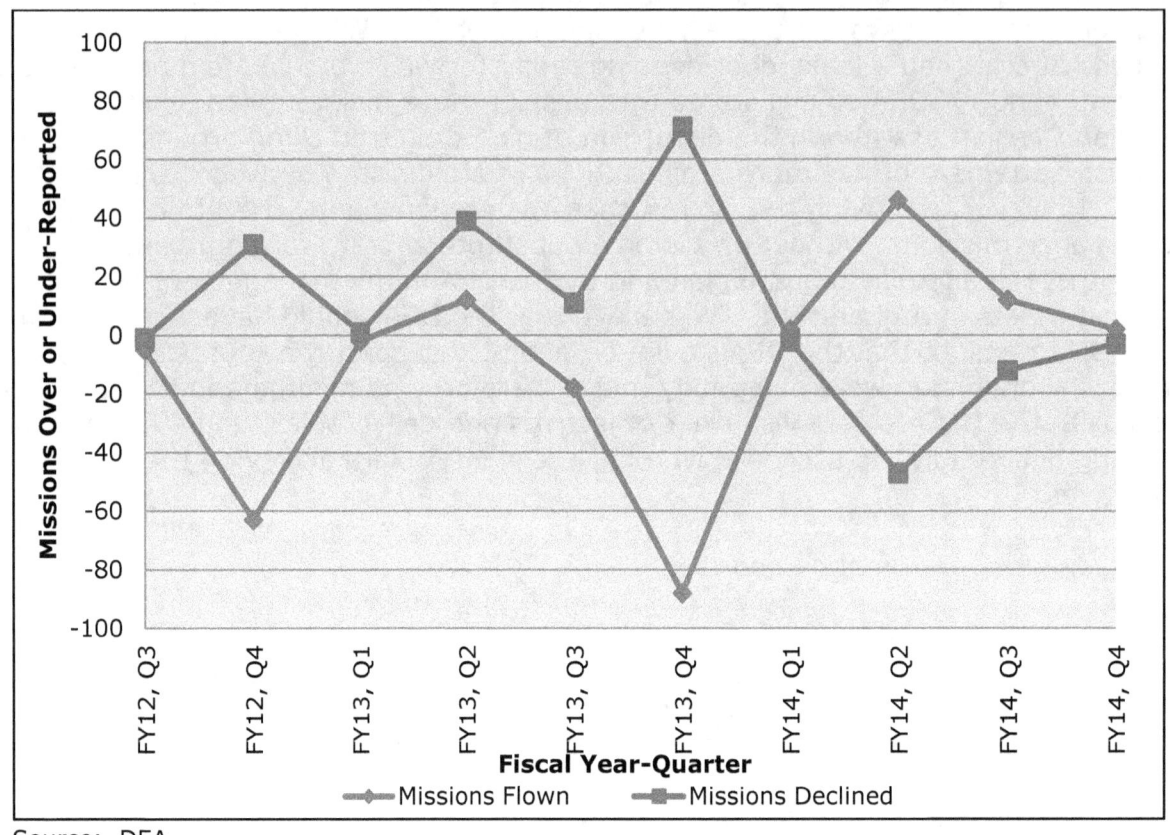

Source: DEA

When we asked the DEA about the discrepancies, a DEA official explained that the pilots in Afghanistan originally filled out a hardcopy mission report form, which was sent back and entered into a database at the Aviation Operations Center in Fort Worth, Texas. Then, in October 2012, the DEA upgraded its database to Microsoft SharePoint, which allows pilots in Afghanistan to submit mission reports electronically. The Afghanistan Group Supervisor manually counts the mission report forms he has approved in SharePoint and enters those counts onto an electronic spreadsheet in Excel for the purpose of preparing the quarterly report. A DEA official explained that, typos or transpositions, such as counting a mission request that was declined as a mission flown or vice versa, may have occurred during this process. During this discussion, the DEA official informed us that SharePoint has the ability to track mission types and generate division wide reports reflecting further detail of the types of missions performed, which we believe would likely have resulted in more accurate quarterly reports. We recommend that the DEA establish procedures to ensure the programmatic data provided to the DOD is accurate.

Conclusion

We believe that the more than $86 million spent on the purchase and modification of the DEA's ATR 500 aircraft with advanced surveillance capabilities to support the DEA's counternarcotics mission in Afghanistan has been an ineffective and wasteful use of government resources. As one of the two key stakeholders in the Global Discovery program, the DEA failed to properly oversee and protect its interests and those of the American taxpayer, and to ensure the program met established timelines, goals and objectives, and anticipated costs.

When the Global Discovery program began in 2008, the anticipated cost for the Global Discovery program was $22 million with an intended delivery date of December 2012. We found that the DEA purchased an aircraft for nearly $8.6 million without ensuring it was the most cost-effective means to accomplish operational needs. In addition, its purchase of the aircraft did not fully comply with the terms and conditions established in its solicitation and the provisions of the FAR. Therefore, we question the DEA's purchase of the ATR 500 for $8,572,638. Further, the DEA transferred the ATR 500 to the DOD's contractors without any documentation of record and without a written agreement with the DOD as to the parameters of the Global Discovery program to ensure that the major modifications agreed upon were performed in a timely and proper fashion. As of March 2016, modifications to the aircraft are still in process, the plane has never flown in Afghanistan, and it is currently in an un-flyable state. In addition, the DEA has expended approximately $8.5 million on parts for the ATR 500, the majority of which cannot be utilized on any other aircraft in its fleet; and the DOD built a hangar in Afghanistan, at a cost of almost $2 million, specifically designed for the plane that it has never housed and likely never will. The current date for completion of the Global Discovery program is June 2016; nearly 1 year after the DEA removed its aviation assets from Afghanistan. The DEA has indicated that, once completed, it plans to utilize the plane elsewhere. We have referred all findings pertaining to the DOD's role in the Global Discovery program to the DOD's Office of Inspector General.

We also found that the DEA did not comply with the terms and conditions of the MOUs that it entered into with the DOD. Specifically, we found that the DEA diverted $2,383,193 for Global Discovery program related expenditures, and charged travel-related expenditures for non-Afghanistan operations, training unrelated to Afghanistan, and other unallowable expenditures. In addition, the DEA charged $78,208 to the MOUs in unsupported non-personnel costs. Furthermore, we determined that the DEA did not ensure that the MOUs it entered into with the DOD identified clear objectives and deliverables. Without such established deliverables and an accurate method to track performance, the DEA was unable to perform a meaningful review and analysis of its operations in Afghanistan. Finally, based on the data available to us, particularly regarding the DEA's inefficient use of its aviation assets in Afghanistan, coupled with the number of mission requests declined by the DEA and the number of missions performed by other agencies; our findings raise serious questions as to whether the DEA was able to meet the operational needs for which its presence was requested in Afghanistan.

Recommendations

We recommend that the DEA:

1. Remedy $8,572,638 in questioned costs for the procurement of the ATR 500 aircraft by strengthening internal controls to ensure existing policies and procedures are followed and that it abides by federal acquisition regulations in its solicitation and procurement process when purchasing future aircraft.

2. Ensure that the parts for the ATR 500 are utilized or returned to the DOD.

3. Ensure that major agreements involving the transfer or modification of high-dollar assets, such as aircraft, be sufficiently documented to provide a record of the transfer, the terms and conditions related to any agreements pertaining to the assets that are being transferred, and any modifications that are to be completed, as well as the responsibility and time frame therefor; and remedial provisions to protect the interests of the DEA in the event of loss or damage that may occur to the DEA's assets during that process.

4. Remedy $2,335,740 in unallowable non-personnel expenditures charged to the MOUs including:

   a. Remedy $1,664,699 in unallowable non-personnel expenditures that the DEA has incorrectly claimed for maintenance of the Global Discovery ATR 500 aircraft, travel to oversee the Global Discovery program, and training for pilots and mechanics to fly the ATR 500.

   b. Remedy $671,041 in unallowable non-personnel expenditures that the DEA has incorrectly claimed for travel-related expenditures for non-Afghanistan operations, training unrelated to Afghanistan, and other unallowable expenditures.

5. Remedy the $78,208 in unsupported non-personnel expenditures charged to the MOUs including:

   a. Remedy $26,262 in unsupported non-personnel expenditures that the DEA claimed for training, maintenance of aircraft, travel, and other unsupported expenditures.

   b. Remedy the $51,946 in unsupported non-personnel expenditures that the DEA claimed for electricity and generator services at Camp Alvarado, located at the Kabul International Airport.

6. Establish procedures to ensure the Aviation Division adheres to its policy requiring that training records be maintained in sufficient detail for both the DEA and contract personnel.

7. Ensure that the Kabul Country Office follows the DEA's policy for maintaining obligation and payment support documentation in UFMS to ensure the goods and services charged from other agencies are accurate, supported, and allowable.

8. Strengthen its internal controls by establishing procedures on how it oversees and verifies the Aviation Division's contractor's performance, to ensure that contractors provide adequate support for the charges that are billed to the DEA and that the DEA review supporting documentation prior to paying summary monthly invoices.

9. Remedy the $47,453 in unallowable personnel expenditures charged to the MOUs.

10. Put the $262,102 of MOU funds intended for ATR 500 maintenance to a better use.

11. Ensure the MOUs it enters into with the DOD have suitable dates for all required financial reporting.

12. Work with the DOD to establish clear objectives and deliverables, and a method for tracking deliverables to ascertain whether these efforts are achieving the desired objectives.

13. Establish procedures to ensure programmatic data provided to the DOD is accurate.

STATEMENT ON INTERNAL CONTROLS

As required by Government Auditing Standards, we tested, as appropriate, internal controls significant within the context of our audit objectives. A deficiency in an internal control exists when the design or operation of a control does not allow management or employees, in the normal course of performing their assigned functions, to timely prevent, or detect: (1) impairments to the effectiveness or efficiency of operations; (2) misstatements in financial or performance information, or (3) violations of laws and regulations. Our evaluation of the DEA's internal controls was *not* made for the purpose of providing assurance on its internal control structure as a whole. The DEA's management is responsible for the establishment and maintenance of internal controls.

As noted in the Findings and Recommendations section of this report, we identified deficiencies in the DEA's internal controls that are significant within the context of the audit objectives and based upon the audit work performed that we believe adversely affect the DEA's ability to ensure compliance with all rules, regulations, policy and procedures for receiving, reviewing, and paying contractor invoices for personnel costs charged to the MOUs. Also, we found that the DEA needs to implement policies and procedures to ensure it fully abides by federal acquisition regulations in its solicitation and procurement process when purchasing aircraft. Additionally, the DEA needs to implement a policy to ensure that MOUs it enters into have established objectives and deliverables and ensure those deliverables are being met and tracked.

Because we are not expressing an opinion on the DEA's internal control structure as a whole, this statement is intended solely for the information and use of the DEA. This restriction is not intended to limit the distribution of this report, which is a matter of public record.

STATEMENT ON COMPLIANCE WITH LAWS AND REGULATIONS

As required by the *Government Auditing Standards* we tested, as appropriate given our audit scope and objectives, selected transactions, records, procedures, and practices, to obtain reasonable assurance that the Drug Enforcement Administration's (DEA) management complied with federal laws and regulations, for which noncompliance, in our judgment, could have a material effect on the results of our audit. The DEA's management is responsible for ensuring compliance with applicable federal laws and regulations. In planning our audit, we identified the following laws and regulations that concerned the operations of the auditee and that were significant within the context of the audit objectives:

- Federal Acquisition Regulation (FAR)

- U.S. Economy Act (31 U.S.C. §1535)

- National Defense Authorization Act of 1991 (Pub. L. No 101-510)

Our audit included examining, on a test basis, the DEA's compliance with the aforementioned laws and regulations that could have a material effect on the DEA's operations, through interviewing DEA officials and its contract personnel, analyzing financial and programmatic data, assessing internal control procedures, and examining procedural practices. As noted in the Findings and Recommendations section of this report, we found instances where the DEA did not have sufficient controls in place to ensure full compliance with the FAR. Specifically, the DEA did not fully comply with the FAR in its procurement of an aircraft for the Global Discovery program including: (1) providing a brand name justification along with the solicitation; (2) ensuring that legitimate needs were identified and trade-offs evaluated and that market research was conducted; and (3) ensuring all bids submitted were evaluated based on the factors and sub-factors contained in the solicitation.

OBJECTIVES, SCOPE, AND METHODOLOGY

Audit Objectives

The primary objective of our audit was to assess the Drug Enforcement Administration's (DEA) Global Discovery program and compliance with the Memoranda of Understanding (MOUs) DEA entered into with the Department of Defense (DOD) supporting DEA's aviation operations in Afghanistan.

Scope and Methodology Section

We conducted this performance audit in accordance with generally accepted government auditing standards. Those standards require that we plan and perform the audit to obtain sufficient, appropriate evidence to provide a reasonable basis for our findings and conclusions based on our audit objectives. We believe that the evidence obtained provides a reasonable basis for our findings and conclusions based on our audit objectives.

This was an audit of the DEA's Global Discovery program and MOUs with the DOD to support aviation operations in Afghanistan. Our audit generally covered, but was not limited to, October 1, 2012, through November 1, 2014; and the entities included in our audit are listed in Appendix 3.

To accomplish our objective we performed work at DEA headquarters in Arlington, Virginia, and at the DEA Aviation Operations Center in Fort Worth, Texas. We conducted interviews with DEA's Chief Financial Officer, Aviation Division Special Agent in Charge, Group Supervisor at the Kabul Country Office, and other DEA officials and personnel. Additionally, we interviewed DOD personnel in charge of the Global Discovery program and DOD financial office personnel with knowledge about the MOUs. We also visited the facility that houses the ATR 500 aircraft and interviewed the contractor and subcontractor personnel for the Global Discovery program. We did not travel to Afghanistan as part of this audit.

Because the DEA was one of two primary stakeholders in the Global Discovery program, our audit focused on the DEA's role in the Global Discovery program. Specifically, we assessed the timeliness and reasonableness of the aircraft modification, the allowability of the DEA's expenditures, and whether the DEA's expenditures were sufficiently supported. In determining whether the DEA properly used Global Discovery program funding, we reviewed the ATR 500 aircraft purchase contract, assessed whether the DEA's procurement of the aircraft was in compliance with the Federal Acquisition Regulation, and evaluated the DEA's methodology for selecting an aircraft for purchase. We also reviewed the DEA's costs associated with the Global Discovery program to ensure that the costs were allowable, supported, and in accordance with applicable laws, regulations, and terms and conditions of the MOUs.

To ensure the DEA's compliance with the terms and conditions of the MOUs it entered into with the DOD, our review consisted of: (1) assessing whether the DEA's activities were in compliance with the requirements and intent of the MOUs; (2) determining if the DEA was meeting the goals and objectives contained in the MOUs; and (3) reviewing the DEA's expenditures on aviation operations in Afghanistan in relation to the MOUs. We reviewed the DEA's MOUs with the DOD to determine if the whistleblower allegation, that the DEA has misused DOD funding by misdirecting, diverting, and spending it for purposes unrelated to supporting the DEA's two aircraft operating in Afghanistan, had any indication of merit.

To evaluate whether costs charged to the MOUs were allowable, supported, and in accordance with applicable laws, regulations, and terms and conditions of the MOUs, we judgmentally selected a sample of 94 out of 871 expenditures between FYs 2012 and 2015, totaling $15,419,897 of the $21,798,038 expended as of February 2015. Among them, we tested non-personnel expenditures totaling $14,228,935, which consisted of operation and maintenance costs of aircraft in Afghanistan, TDY costs for DEA personnel and contractors traveling to and from Afghanistan, training, parts purchased for the ATR 500, and electricity and generator maintenance at Camp Alvarado in Kabul, Afghanistan. We also tested personnel costs totaling $1,190,961, which included direct labor, special pays and bonuses paid to contractor pilots and mechanics to support the DEA's aviation operations in Afghanistan. For these sampled expenditures, we reviewed supporting documentation, tested calculations, and reviewed pertinent DEA manuals and policies to determine if they were adequately supported and properly charged to the MOUs. The non-statistical sample design does not allow a projection of the test results for all expenditures or internal controls and procedures.

Specifically, we reviewed the DEA's submission of financial and programmatic reports to the DOD during FYs 2012 through 2014, as these reports were the basis for the DEA's requests for reimbursement. We determined whether these reports were accurate and submitted timely. We also reviewed unobligated funds for each of the MOUs to determine if funds were returned to the DOD before the end of the fiscal year. To assess the impact of the DEA's use of MOU funds on its counternarcotics efforts in Afghanistan, we reviewed the DEA's mission reports for fiscal years 2012 through 2015. We analyzed the number and types of missions flown in the DEA's mission reports and compared those numbers to the programmatic information that the DEA provided to the DOD to determine the accuracy of the information that the DEA was reporting to the DOD. We also evaluated the number of missions completed and declined to determine if the DEA was able to keep pace with aviation operational needs in Afghanistan. Specifically, we assessed the availability of the DEA's surveillance aircraft in Afghanistan to determine whether it was impacting the DEA's overall mission in Afghanistan.

We did not assess the DOD's oversight, management, or funding related to the Global Discovery program. Any findings that we identified during our review that were particular to the DOD's oversight were referred to the DOD Office of Inspector General.

SCHEDULE OF DOLLAR-RELATED FINDINGS

Description	Amount	Page
Unallowable Cost:		
Unallowable procurement of the ATR 500 aircraft	$8,572,638	9
Unallowable MOU costs on training, travel, and maintenance of the ATR 500	1,664,699	25
Unallowable Non-Personnel Expenditures charged to the MOUs	671,041	21
Unallowable Personnel Expenditures charged to the MOUs	47,453	25
Total Unallowable Costs	**$10,955,831**	
Unsupported Costs:		
Unsupported Non-Personnel Expenditures charged to the MOUs	$78,208	22
Total Unsupported Costs	**$78,208**	
Funds Put to Better Use[36]	**$262,102**	26
Gross Questioned Costs[37]	**$11,296,141**	
Less Duplication	($11,676)	
Net Questioned Costs	**$11,284,465**	

[36] Funds put to better use are future funds that could be used more efficiently if management took actions to implement and complete audit recommendations. This definition is based on provisions within the Inspector General Act of 1978, as amended, codified as 5 U.S.C. 3 § 5(f)(4) (1978).

[37] Questioned costs are expenditures that do not comply with legal, regulatory, or contractual requirements, or are not supported by adequate documentation at the time of the audit, or are unnecessary or unreasonable. Questioned costs may be remedied by offset, waiver, recovery of funds, or the provision of supporting documentation.

ENTITIES FOR THE MOUS WITH THE DOD AND GLOBAL DISCOVERY PROGRAM

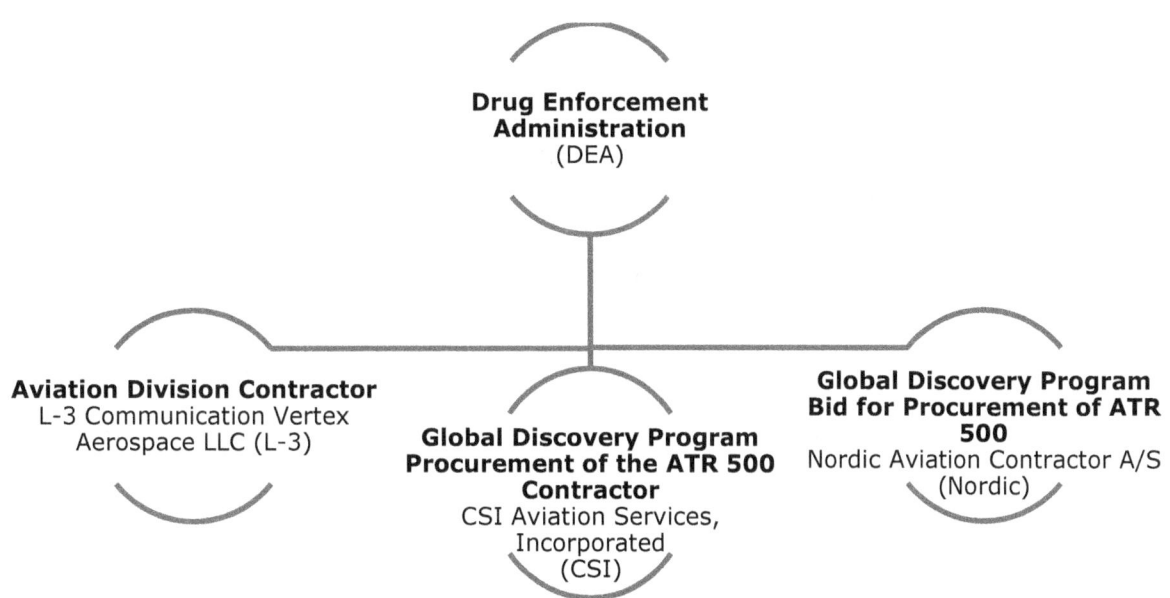

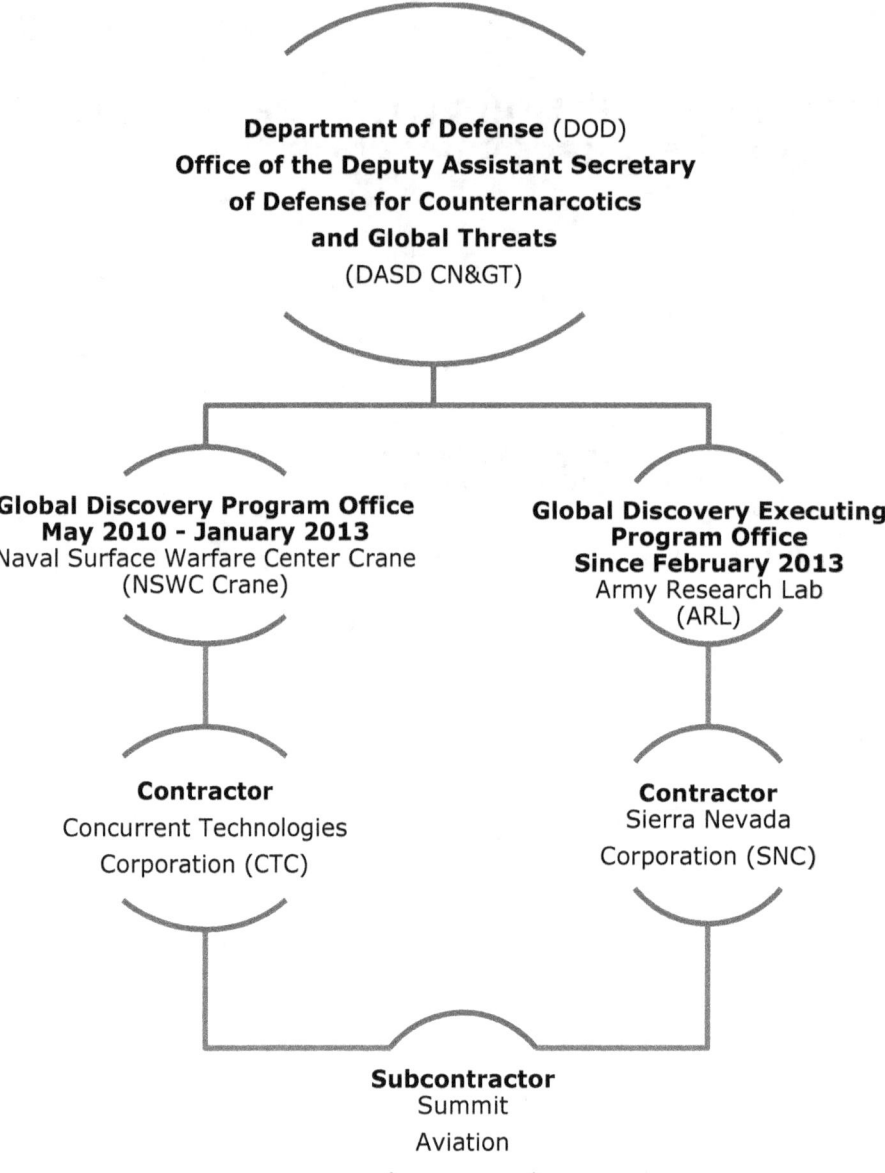

Department of Defense (DOD)
Office of the Deputy Assistant Secretary
of Defense for Counternarcotics
and Global Threats
(DASD CN&GT)

Global Discovery Program Office
May 2010 - January 2013
Naval Surface Warfare Center Crane
(NSWC Crane)

Global Discovery Executing
Program Office
Since February 2013
Army Research Lab
(ARL)

Contractor
Concurrent Technologies
Corporation (CTC)

Contractor
Sierra Nevada
Corporation (SNC)

Subcontractor
Summit
Aviation

THE DRUG ENFORCEMENT ADMINISTRATION'S
RESPONSE TO THE DRAFT AUDIT REPORT

U. S. Department of Justice
Drug Enforcement Administration

www.dea.gov   Washington, D.C. 20537

MAR 1 7 2016

MEMORANDUM

TO: David Gaschke
              Regional Audit Manager
              San Francisco Regional Audit Office
              Office of the Inspector General

FROM: Michael J. Stanfill
              Deputy Chief Inspector
              Office of Inspections

SUBJECT: DEA Response for the OIG Draft Report: _"Audit of the Drug Enforcement
              Administration's Aviation Operations with the Department of Defense in
              Afghanistan"_

The Drug Enforcement Administration (DEA) has reviewed the Department of Justice (DOJ)
Office of the Inspector General's (OIG) Draft Report entitled, _"Audit of the Drug Enforcement
Administration's Aviation Operations with the Department of Defense in Afghanistan."_ DEA
provides the following response to the draft report.

General Comments

The report takes issue with a broad range of items to include: the purchase of the ATR 500;
DEA's use of Department of Defense (DoD) funds for DEA aviation operations in support of
counternarcotics efforts in Afghanistan; the accounting systems utilized by the DEA Aviation
Division's maintenance support contractor; the DEA Aviation Division's training records; and the
effectiveness of DEA aviation operations in Afghanistan. Several of OIG's assessments merit
contextualization or clarification.

In September 2008, DEA purchased an ATR 500 aircraft to support our counternarcotics efforts
in Afghanistan. In January 2011, DEA sought, under the authority of Section 1004 of the National
Defense Authorization Act of 1991, funding for the necessary and appropriate modifications of the
ATR 500 aircraft, which became known as the Global Discovery program. Due to DEA's
longstanding and exceptional relationship with DoD, DEA requested that "DoD provide program
funding, program management, and executive oversight of the Global Discovery modification." In

April 2011, DEA requested, under the same authority, funding to support its aviation operations in Afghanistan and subsequently entered into a Memorandum of Understanding (MOU) with DoD in November of that year.

DEA had previous positive experiences utilizing DoD contractors for modifying DEA aircraft. Several DEA aircraft had received modifications through other DoD programs responsible for sustainment and modification of specialized aircraft. The significant difference between previous aircraft modifications and the Global Discovery program was that in the previous modifications, DEA utilized its own funding and, therefore, had the latitude to be more involved in the modification process. Based upon that previous experience, DEA had no indication that the Global Discovery modification would encounter the significant delays and problems that ultimately occurred.

DEA takes exception to some of the assessments made throughout the report. Some of the language utilized in the report inaccurately depicts actions taken by DEA's Aviation Division. The use of the term "divert" when referencing the utilization of MOU funds toward the Global Discovery program implies a willful intent to expend the funds in a manner for which they were not intended. Any use by DEA of MOU funding for the Global Discovery program occurred with the understanding that it was fully supported by DoD and consistent with the MOU's parameters.

Additionally, many of the audit report conclusions have been based upon OIG's interpretation of the intent of the MOU between DEA and DoD. The "Authority and Purpose" section of the MOU, states "DoD agrees to provide funding under the terms set forth in this MOU pending the availability of funds and statutory authority under Section 1004. DEA will use the funding provided pursuant to the MOU to continue the operations of the DEA Aviation detachment in support of the Government of Afghanistan." DEA understood that under the MOU, funding could be used to support aviation operations in Afghanistan. Further, DEA remained in regular contact with DoD regarding all matters involving the MOU, including this interpretation about the use of funding. DEA has provided OIG with verbal explanations and written documentation between DEA and DoD concerning that interpretation. Despite that information, OIG has continued to deem specific expenses as unallowable and states DEA diverted funds from the MOU based upon OIG's narrow interpretation of the MOU. DEA continues to disagree with OIG's interpretation on this point and believes that the available information shows otherwise.

Recommendations

The OIG makes 13 recommendations in the report. Below are DEA's responses to the recommendations.

Recommendation 1: Remedy $8,572,638 in questioned costs for the procurement of the ATR 500 aircraft by strengthening internal controls to ensure existing policies and procedures are followed and that it abides by federal acquisition regulations in its solicitation and procurement process when purchasing future aircraft.

DEA Response

DEA concurs with the recommendation. The OIG acknowledged in its report that DEA implemented additional internal controls since the purchase of the ATR. Standard Operating Acquisition Procedure (SOAP) 2011-04 established a Contract Review Board (CRB) to implement a formal process and procedure for obtaining oversight and advisory review of significant contract actions. The purpose of the CRB review is to ensure compliance with the Federal Acquisition Regulations and other legal requirements, adherence to DEA and DOJ policy and procedural guidance, conformity to acquisition best practices, soundness of acquisition strategy, sufficiency and appropriateness of the requirement description (i.e., statements of work, specifications, and similar items), allowance of competition to the maximum extent practicable, appropriateness of sourcing considerations, and other matters. DEA has issued further guidance to ensure compliance of these existing policies. Additionally, DEA will routinely reassess its policy for further enhancements and improvements. Documents in support of this recommendation have been provided under separate cover.

Based on the above information, DEA requests closure of this recommendation.

Recommendation 2: Ensure that the parts for the ATR 500 are utilized or returned to the DOD.

DEA Response

DEA concurs with the recommendation. Dependent upon the final outcome of the aircraft modifications, DEA will either utilize or dispose of the parts for the ATR 500 in compliance with DoD's guidance and all appropriate regulations.

Recommendation 3: Ensure that major agreements involving the transfer or modification of high-dollar assets, such as aircraft, be sufficiently documented to provide a record of the transfer, the terms and conditions related to any agreements pertaining to the assets that are being transferred, and any modifications that are to be completed, as well as the responsibility and time frame therefor; and remedial provisions to protect the interests of the DEA in the event of loss or damage that may occur to the DEA's assets during that process.

DEA Response

DEA does not concur with this recommendation as written. DEA disagrees with the terminology utilized by OIG as its aircraft are never transferred to contractors or subcontractors for maintenance or modification, as the term "transfer" indicates a change of ownership. Aviation industry standards do not require a record of transfer for the purposes of maintenance or modification. Rather, the aircraft is inducted into maintenance and an induction checklist is completed and becomes a part of the aircraft's maintenance records. DEA will continue to comply with industry standards in this regard when aircraft are inducted into routine maintenance or modifications; however, in the future, DEA will comply with the spirit of this recommendation and require more detailed documentation in the event it is inducting an aircraft into a major modification through an MOU, such as the Global Discovery program.

Recommendation 4: Remedy $2,335,740 in unallowable non-personnel expenditures charged to the MOUs including:

    a. Remedy $1,664,699 in unallowable non-personnel expenditures that the DEA has incorrectly claimed for maintenance of the Global Discovery ATR 500 aircraft, travel to oversee the Global Discovery program, and training for pilots and mechanics to fly the ATR 500.

    b. Remedy $671,041 in unallowable non-personnel expenditures that the DEA has incorrectly claimed for travel-related expenditures for non-Afghanistan operations, training unrelated to Afghanistan, and other unallowable expenditures.

<u>DEA Response</u>

In order to resolve and close this recommendation, DEA requests a final analysis of the remaining expenditures deemed to be unallowable so that reviews can be conducted. While DEA disagrees with OIG's assessment of its analysis of DoD funds for aviation support to Afghanistan, DEA will make every effort to address the items identified as unallowable. DEA acknowledges that, as with any program, human error may have occurred in the application of some of the expenditures. Reviews conducted during the course of this audit have attempted to identify and rectify erroneous billings. DEA will document the steps taken to remedy anything determined to be erroneous. Moving forward, DEA will ensure that future MOUs provide more specific language regarding the parameters for utilization of funding.

Recommendation 5: Remedy the $78,208 in unsupported non-personnel expenditures charged to the MOUs including:

    a.   Remedy $26,262 in unsupported non-personnel expenditures that the DEA claimed for training, maintenance of aircraft, travel, and other unsupported expenditures.

    b.   Remedy the $51,946 in unsupported non-personnel expenditures that the DEA claimed for electricity and generator services at Camp Alvarado, located at the Kabul International Airport.

<u>DEA Response</u>

In order to resolve and close this recommendation, DEA requests a final analysis of the remaining expenditures deemed to be unsupported so reviews can be conducted. DEA will then document the steps taken to remedy anything determined to be erroneous. DEA will also ensure proper documentation is maintained as justification for expenses.

Recommendation 6: Establish procedures to ensure the Aviation Division adheres to its policy requiring that training records be maintained in sufficient detail for both the DEA and contract personnel.

DEA Response

DEA concurs with the recommendation. This recommendation primarily refers to a training course for which the vendor did not provide the Aviation Division or employees with a certificate of completion. To satisfy this recommendation, the Aviation Division will generate documentation showing that an employee has completed a training course in which the vendor does not provide a certificate of completion.

Recommendation 7: Ensure that the Kabul Country Office follows the DEA's policy for maintaining obligation and payment support documentation in UFMS to ensure the goods and services charged from other agencies are accurate, supported, and allowable.

DEA Response

DEA concurs with the recommendation. In prior years, DEA identified through internal reviews that foreign offices had difficulty providing supporting documentation in a timely manner for goods and services procured by the State Department on behalf of DEA. In response to this concern, the Office of Finance (FN) established new policy in October 2014, which required foreign offices to scan and attach obligation and payment support documentation into Unified Financial Management System (UFMS) for goods and services procured by the State Department on behalf of DEA. To confirm compliance with this new requirement, FN performed sample reviews of obligations and associated transactions processed through the State Department beginning in January 2015, to validate the completeness of the scanned and attached support documentation in UFMS. The results of the reviews indicated that while compliance has improved, some foreign offices continued to struggle. In order to provide more support to the foreign offices, FN established a Foreign Review and Monitoring Team in November 2015, to continuously review, identify, correct, and monitor financial transactions and operations in the foreign offices. Documents in support of this recommendation have been provided under separate cover.

Based on this information, DEA requests closure of the recommendation.

Recommendation 8: Strengthen its internal controls by establishing procedures on how it oversees and verifies the Aviation Division's contractor's performance, to ensure that contractors provide adequate support for the charges that are billed to the DEA and that the DEA review supporting documentation prior to paying summary monthly invoices.

DEA Response

DEA concurs with the recommendation. DEA will strengthen its internal controls related to invoice processing. The Contracting Officer Representatives (COR) will be issued further guidance to ensure compliance of existing DEA policies. Verification of Receipt and Acceptance forms will be completed in UFMS on each invoice. The COR will review and/or cross check any supporting documentation included with each invoice. Copies of such documents will be retained in the COR file for review and auditing purposes. The COR will develop and implement procedures for ensuring random samples are reviewed at a minimum on a quarterly basis. Additionally, during the formal closeouts of these contracts, a Defense Contract Management Agency (DCMA) audit will be performed to ensure all charges were allowable and allocable to the contract.

Recommendation 9: Remedy the $47,453 in unallowable personnel expenditures charged to the MOUs.

<u>DEA Response</u>

DEA does not have sufficient information to concur with this recommendation. This recommendation pertains to alleged overbillings regarding direct labor charges and special pay by the Aviation Division's maintenance support contractor, L-3. L-3 attempted to explain the shared services system it utilizes and the manner in which pay was calculated based upon personnel rotation schedules. Due to the rotations of personnel and the fact that these rotations did not occur in concert with billing and pay period start and end dates, it is virtually impossible to reconcile the billings without assessing them in a year-long time frame. L-3 has conducted an internal review of many of the items provided and is continuing to do so. Any items identified as being erroneous will be addressed by L-3. As stated in Federal Acquisition Regulation 42.101, the DCMA is the responsible government audit agency that performs final audits on all contract periods in which any remaining errors are identified and subsequently addressed.

Recommendation 10: Put the $262,102 of MOU funds intended for ATR 500 maintenance to a better use.

<u>DEA Response</u>

DEA cannot concur with this recommendation. This recommendation pertains to funding that has been obligated toward work performed on the ATR. As the work has already been performed and the funding obligated for that expense, the Aviation Division is unable to put the funding to any other use.

Based on this information, DEA requests closure of this recommendation.

Recommendation 11: Ensure the MOUs it enters into with the DOD have suitable dates for all required financial reporting.

<u>DEA Response</u>

DEA concurs with the recommendation. The Office of Resource Management has developed a training presentation that will ensure DEA personnel fully understand the terms on all MOUs. The training presentation has been provided under separate cover.

Based on this information, DEA requests closure of this recommendation.

Recommendation 12: Work with the DOD to establish clear objectives and deliverables, and a method for tracking deliverables to ascertain whether these efforts are achieving the desired objectives.

<u>DEA Response</u>

DEA concurs with this recommendation. For any future MOUs with DoD, DEA, as a participant, will make every effort to ensure that mutually agreeable objectives and deliverables are reflected in clear and specific language. DEA will work with DoD to determine the end stated goals for the MOUs and the mutually agreed upon metrics by which these goals should be accomplished.

Recommendation 13: Establish procedures to ensure programmatic data provided to the DOD is accurate.

<u>DEA Response</u>

DEA concurs with the recommendation. The Aviation Division has established an electronic submission of mission reports which will simplify the process for providing programmatic data to DoD and ensure its accuracy. Documents in support of this recommendation have been provided under separate cover.

If you have any questions regarding this response, please contact the Audit Liaison Team, on 202-307-8200.

OFFICE OF THE INSPECTOR GENERAL
ANALYSIS AND SUMMARY OF ACTIONS
NECESSARY TO RESOLVE THE REPORT

The Office of the Inspector General (OIG) provided a draft of this audit report to the Drug Enforcement Administration (DEA). The DEA's response is incorporated into Appendix 4 of this final report. The following provides the OIG analysis of the response and summary of actions necessary to resolve the report.

Analysis of the DEA's Response

In response to our audit, the DEA did not concur with all of our recommendations. As a result, the status of the audit report is unresolved.

The DEA stated in its response that it takes exception to some of the assessments made throughout the report. Specifically, the DEA stated that any use of Memoranda of Understanding (MOU) funds by the DEA for the Global Discovery program occurred with the understanding that it was fully supported by the DOD and consistent with the MOU parameters. The DEA also stated that many of our report conclusions have been based upon the OIG's own interpretation of the intent of the MOUs between the DEA and the DOD. We disagree with these statements. Our conclusions and recommendations described in our report were based on evidence we obtained during the course of our audit.

The MOUs for aviation operations in Afghanistan, specifically to support the DEA's two Beech King Air 350's, clearly state that the, "DEA will use the funding provided pursuant to the MOU to continue the operations of the DEA Aviation detachment in support of the Government of Afghanistan." As of March 2016, the DEA's Global Discovery aircraft has never flown in Afghanistan; and therefore, the expenditures the DEA charged related to the Global Discovery program and other non-Afghanistan aviation operations violated the terms and conditions of the MOUs.

Further, the DEA provided documentation of its request to the DOD asking to use MOU funding intended for aviation operations on-going in Afghanistan in order to repair the Global Discovery program's ATR 500 to its original flying condition. A DOD official responded that the MOU funds can only be used for aviation operations in Afghanistan and requested that the DEA make a separate request to use alternate funding for requests related to the Global Discovery program and the DEA's ATR 500. We were not informed of any separate request.

Summary of Actions Necessary to Resolve the Report

1. **Remedy $8,572,638 in questioned costs for the procurement of the ATR 500 aircraft by strengthening internal controls to ensure existing policies and procedures are followed and that it abides by**

federal acquisition regulations in its solicitation and procurement process when purchasing future aircraft.

Resolved. The DEA concurred with our recommendation. The DEA stated that in 2011, the DEA's Standard Operating Acquisition Procedure established the Contract Review Board to implement a formal process and procedure for obtaining oversight and advisory review of significant contract actions. As part of its response, the DEA provided to the OIG a March 2016 memorandum issued to its Office of Acquisition and Relocation Management, reminding staff to adhere to the procedures established through the Contract Review Board and the DEA's Standard Operating Acquisition Procedure. The memorandum states that subject matter experts will provide advisory review to Contracting Officers for significant contract actions and ensure that acquisitions comply with legal requirements and adhere to federal, departmental, and local policies. The DEA also stated an updated Standard Operating Acquisition Procedure is being created and will be shared with DEA staff once it is implemented. This recommendation can be closed once documentation of the DEA's updated Standard Operating Acquisition Procedure has been issued and implemented, and a copy has been provided to the OIG for its review.

2. **Ensure that the parts for the ATR 500 are utilized or returned to the DOD.**

   Resolved. The DEA concurred with our recommendation. The DEA stated that it will either utilize or dispose of the parts for the aircraft in compliance with the DOD's guidance and all appropriate regulations, dependent upon the final outcome of the ATR 500's modifications. This recommendation can be closed when the DEA provides documentation to support that the parts have either been: (1) utilized by a DEA Federal Aviation Administration certified air-worthy ATR 500 aircraft, or (2) returned to the DOD in a manner that is consistent with the DOD's guidance and all appropriate regulations.

3. **Ensure that major agreements involving the transfer or modification of high-dollar assets, such as aircraft, be sufficiently documented to provide a record of the transfer, the terms and conditions related to any agreements pertaining to the assets that are being transferred, and any modifications that are to be completed, as well as the responsibility and time frame therefor; and remedial provisions to protect the interests of the DEA in the event of loss or damage that may occur to the DEA's assets during that process.**

   Resolved. Although the DEA stated that it did not concur with the recommendation due to its disagreement with our use of the word "transfer," it also stated that it will comply with the spirit of the recommendation and described corrective actions that reflect its agreement with the recommendation in principle. Therefore, we have determined that this resolves this recommendation.

The DEA expressed the view that the word transfer, in the context of discussing aircraft, indicates a change of ownership and is not used when referring to routine maintenance or modification. Rather, according to the DEA, an aircraft is inducted into maintenance and an induction checklist is completed and becomes a part of the aircraft's maintenance records. For the purpose of this report, the OIG's use of the term transfer is used to indicate the movement of the DEA's aircraft from one place to another. Nevertheless, the DEA has not provided any documentation, including an induction checklist, for the DEA ATR 500's induction to the DOD subcontractor's facility for modification.

For the future, the DEA also stated that it will require more detailed documentation in the event it is inducting an aircraft into a major modification, such as the Global Discovery program, through an MOU. Keeping detailed records pertaining to the modification of high-dollar assets, regardless of whether that asset is part of an MOU, is essential to the effective oversight and management of that asset. As we discuss in this report, the DEA has had difficulty ensuring that all agreed upon modifications were made to the ATR 500 and it has failed to hold the DOD accountable for timely completion of the project. The aircraft, purchased over 7 years ago, has missed every intended delivery date, and the current expected delivery date is June 2016.

This recommendation can be closed when we receive documentation indicating that the DEA has taken steps to ensure that major agreements involving the transfer, induction, or modification of high-dollar assets, such as aircraft, are sufficiently documented to provide a record of the transfer or induction, the terms and conditions related to any agreements pertaining to the assets that are being transferred or inducted, and any modifications that are to be completed. In addition, the documentation should include the identification of the responsible parties involved and the time frame of the transfer, induction, or modification. Any remedial provisions to protect the interests of the DEA in the event of loss or damage that may occur to the DEA's assets during these processes should also be provided in the documentation.

4. **Remedy $2,335,740 in unallowable non-personnel expenditures charged to the MOUs including:**

   a. **Remedy $1,664,699 in unallowable non-personnel expenditures that the DEA has incorrectly claimed for maintenance of the Global Discovery ATR 500 aircraft, travel to oversee the Global Discovery program, and training for pilots and mechanics to fly the ATR 500.**

   b. **Remedy $671,041 in unallowable non-personnel expenditures that the DEA has incorrectly claimed for travel-related expenditures for**

non-Afghanistan operations, training unrelated to Afghanistan, and other unallowable expenditures.

Resolved. The DEA stated that it will make every effort to address the items identified as unallowable. In its response, the DEA requested a final analysis of the remaining unallowable expenditures so that reviews can be conducted in order to resolve and close this recommendation. During the course of our audit close-out meeting on February 10, 2016, the DEA requested a list of each of the unallowable expenditures related to this recommendation. We provided this information to the DEA on February 11, 2016. The DEA acknowledged that human error may have occurred in the application of some of the expenditures and stated that it will document the steps taken to remedy erroneous expenditures. The DEA further stated that it will ensure that future MOUs provide more specific language regarding the parameters for utilizing MOU funding. This recommendation can be closed when the DEA remedies the $2,335,740 in unallowable non-personnel expenditures charged to the MOUs.

5. **Remedy the $78,208 in unsupported non-personnel expenditures charged to the MOUs including:**

    a. **Remedy $26,262 in unsupported non-personnel expenditures that the DEA claimed for training, maintenance of aircraft, travel, and other unsupported expenditures.**

    b. **Remedy the $51,946 in unsupported non-personnel expenditures that the DEA claimed for electricity and generator services at Camp Alvarado, located at the Kabul International Airport.**

    Resolved. The DEA requested a final analysis of the remaining unsupported expenditures so reviews can be conducted and the recommendation can be resolved and closed. The DEA requested this information during our audit close-out meeting, and we provided it to the DEA the following day. The DEA stated that it will document the steps taken to remedy anything it determines to be erroneous and that it will ensure proper documentation is maintained as justification for expenses. This recommendation can be closed when the DEA remedies the $78,208 in unsupported non-personnel expenditures charged to the MOUs.

6. **Establish procedures to ensure the Aviation Division adheres to its policy requiring that training records be maintained in sufficient detail for both the DEA and contract personnel.**

    Resolved. The DEA concurred with our recommendation. The DEA stated this recommendation primarily refers to a training course for which the vendor did not provide the Aviation Division or its employees with a certificate of completion. As stated on page 23 of this report, this recommendation is the result of $12,875 in unsupported expenditures for 27 required training courses. The DEA stated that it will satisfy this recommendation by having the Aviation Division generate documentation showing that each employee has completed the required training course when the vendor does not provide a certificate of completion. However, this proposed solution does not address the issue we identified during our audit. The problem we identified was not focused on whether the vendor provides certificates of completion, but rather concerned with the DEA's lack of documentation in its training records to reflect course completion. This recommendation can be closed when we receive evidence that the DEA has established procedures to ensure that the Aviation Division adheres to its policy requiring that training records be maintained in sufficient detail for both DEA and contract personnel.

7. **Ensure that the Kabul Country Office follows the DEA's policy for maintaining obligation and payment support documentation in UFMS to ensure the goods and services charged from other agencies are accurate, supported, and allowable.**

    Closed. The DEA concurred with our recommendation and stated that in prior years it had identified, through internal reviews that foreign offices had difficulty providing supporting documentation in a timely manner for goods and services procured by the State Department on behalf of the DEA. In response, the DEA's Office of Finance established a policy in October 2014, requiring foreign offices to scan and attach obligation and payment support documentation into the DEA's Unified Financial Management System (UFMS) for all goods and services procured by the State Department on behalf of DEA. In January 2015, the Office of Finance began performing sample reviews to confirm compliance with the new requirement. The results of the reviews indicated that while compliance had improved, some foreign offices continued to struggle. Therefore, in November 2015, the Office of Finance established a Foreign Review and Monitoring Team to continuously review, identify, correct, and monitor financial transactions and operations in its foreign offices.

    The DEA provided a copy of its Desk Reference Guide, dated January 2016, which contains the new requirement for foreign offices to scan and attach obligation and payment support documentation into UFMS for goods and services procured by the State Department on behalf of the DEA. The DEA also provided a training video on how to properly attach supporting documentation into UFMS, which has been disseminated to its foreign offices for review. Based on the documentation we received from the DEA and its actions to ensure adequate obligation and payment support documentation is maintained in UFMS to support the goods and services charged from the State Department is accurate, supported, and allowable; we consider this recommendation closed.

8. **Strengthen its internal controls by establishing procedures on how it oversees and verifies the Aviation Division's contractor's**

performance, to ensure that contractors provide adequate support for the charges that are billed to the DEA and that the DEA review supporting documentation prior to paying summary monthly invoices.

Resolved. The DEA concurred with our recommendation and stated that it will strengthen its internal controls related to invoice processing and that Contracting Officer's Representatives (COR) will be issued further guidance to ensure compliance with existing DEA policies. Specifically, the DEA stated that verification of receipt and acceptance forms will be completed in UFMS on each invoice and the COR will review and cross check any supporting documentation included with each invoice. The DEA also stated that it will maintain copies of supporting documentation in the COR file for review and auditing purposes. However, it did not specify how long it will maintain this documentation. In addition, the DEA stated that the COR will develop and implement procedures for ensuring random samples are reviewed at a minimum on a quarterly basis. The DEA noted that the Defense Contract Management Agency (DCMA) will also perform an audit to ensure all the charges were allowable and allocable to the contract.

Based on our analysis, however, we determined that the DEA's Aviation Division does not have adequate policies or procedures for receiving, reviewing, and paying contractor invoices for personnel costs. Specifically, the DEA does not require the contractor to list actual pay dates on its invoices to allow a reviewer to cross check the hours billed to the hours worked. Therefore, this recommendation can be closed when we receive evidence that the DEA has established and implemented procedures to strengthen its internal controls for its oversight and verification of Aviation Division contractor's performance, to ensure that contractors provide adequate support for the charges that are billed to the DEA and that the DEA review supporting documentation prior to paying summary monthly invoices.

9. **Remedy the $47,453 in unallowable personnel expenditures charged to the MOUs.**

Resolved. The DEA stated in its response that it does not have sufficient information to agree with this recommendation, but also stated that any items it identifies as erroneous will be addressed by L-3. On multiple occasions during our audit (June and September 2015, and February 2016), we provided the DEA with a current listing of each unallowable personnel expenditure charged to the MOUs. Based on our analysis, the DEA's contactor, L-3 Communications Vertex Aerospace LLC (L-3), has conducted an internal review of many of the items we provided to the DEA and continues to do so. Based on our testing of direct labor and special pay expenditures for the 9 months we reviewed, we found $47,453 in unallowable personnel expenditures charged to the MOUs. This recommendation can be closed when the DEA remedies the remaining $47,453 in unallowable personnel expenditures charged to the MOUs.

10. **Put the $262,102 of MOU funds intended for ATR 500 maintenance to a better use.**

   Unresolved. The DEA stated that it could not concur with this recommendation because the funding has been obligated toward work already performed on the ATR 500, and the Aviation Division is therefore unable to put the funding to any other use. The DEA does not dispute that the funds should be put to better use, but rather that it cannot remedy the expenditure because the funds have already been obligated. However, since the MOU funds from which the DEA intended to pay for maintenance on the ATR 500 are actually meant to support the DEA's aviation operations in Afghanistan, the DEA should de-obligate the current funding for the ATR expense and use the appropriate financial resources to pay for the work that has been performed. Therefore, we maintain that these obligated but not yet expended funds could be put to better use. Should the DEA continue to assert its position or actually expend the funds as currently obligated, based on our finding we anticipate questioning the $262,102 as unallowable costs charged to the MOUs. We consider this recommendation to be unresolved. This recommendation can be resolved and closed once the DEA provides documentation that the $262,102 of MOU funds have been de-obligated from the current expense and put to better use.

11. **Ensure the MOUs it enters into with the DOD have suitable dates for all required financial reporting.**

   Resolved. The DEA concurred with our recommendation and stated that the Office of Resource Management has developed a training presentation that will ensure that DEA personnel fully understand the terms of all MOUs. The DEA provided training material that describes what an MOU is, who in DEA is responsible for vetting MOUs, and guidance on combining an MOU with a reimbursable agreement. The material also reminds staff to be aware of conflicting dollar amounts, dates, and purpose statements within reimbursable agreements and MOUs. The DEA has not yet provided a list of DEA staff required to and who have completed the training. This recommendation can be closed when the DEA provides evidence to ensure that the MOUs it enters into with the DOD have suitable dates for all required financial reporting.

12. **Work with the DOD to establish clear objectives and deliverables, and a method for tracking deliverables to ascertain whether these efforts are achieving the desired objectives.**

   Resolved. The DEA concurred with our recommendation and stated that it will make every effort to ensure that mutually agreeable objectives and deliverables are reflected in clear and specific language for any future MOUs that it enters into with the DOD. The DEA also stated that it will work with the DOD to establish mutually agreed upon metrics by which these goals should be accomplished. The DEA has not yet provided documentation or an explanation as to how it plans to go about ensuring the MOUs it enters into with the DOD have clear objectives and deliverables. Therefore, this recommendation can be closed once we have received evidence that the DEA has worked with the DOD to establish clear objectives and deliverables, and a method for tracking deliverables to ascertain whether these efforts are achieving the desired objectives.

13. **Establish procedures to ensure programmatic data provided to the DOD is accurate.**

Closed. The DEA concurred with our recommendation and stated that it has established an electronic submission of mission reports which will simplify the process for providing programmatic data to the DOD and ensure that it is accurate. As a part of the DEA's response, it provided Division Order 03, which states that Special Agent Pilots will submit mission reports electronically through the DEA's electronic system Concorde. From Concorde, the DEA is able to generate mission reports listed by aircraft, which will improve the DEA's reporting accuracy. Based on the evidence provided by the DEA, we consider this recommendation to be closed.